MYTHS AND TRUTHS OF FINANCIAL PLANNING THROUGHOUT YOUR LIFE

BILL MCBAY, CFP, CLU, CHS, CEA, CFDS

Myths and Truths of Financial Planning Throughout Your Life

ISBN 978-1-9991356-6-9

CONTENTS

LEGAL DISCLOSURE

Legal Disclosure

The tiny print that is always so important.....

This book should not act as anyone's excuse **not** to seek professional advice.

Just because you read this book, it doesn't make your situation equivalent to a 'rule of thumb'. You are unique and so are your finances, goals, thoughts about money and what all that means to you.

The links provided in this book to third party companies or government agencies can change at any time and without warning. Please feel free to Google the information for updates at any time.

The concepts outlined in this book are exactly that, concepts. These, along with many before them and I'm sure many after, are subject to change over time based on product changes, government legislation changes and of course the comfort level of those who use them in their financial planning process.

Governments change regularly and so do the laws and budgets that affect the concepts and information in this book. So stay informed if you plan on doing this yourself or make sure your advisor has processes in place so they stay informed on your behalf.

There are no specific options to purchase products of any nature in this book. If you determine that you wish to purchase financial products that are generally outlined in this book, you must seek out licensed professionals in your area who are educated and experienced in the products you seek.

Everyone has a different level of risk they are comfortable taking on, and this book doesn't consider individual risk factors of those who read the book. That is your job when working with your qualified and experienced financial advisor.

This book doesn't suggest products from one company over another. If a company you are working with doesn't offer the products outlined in this book, this book is not reflecting anything positive or negative against that company.

The only assumption being made of this book is that it is read. Multiple times if necessary or desired.

Not all these concepts are for everyone. You have to do your homework to figure out if they might be for you.

The author of this book is a Certified Financial Planner®, Chartered Life Underwriter®, Certified Health Specialist™, Certified Executor Advisor and Chartered Financial Divorce Specialist, practising in Waterloo, Ontario.

FOREWORD

Financial planning is something everyone talks about, but few make it a priority in their lives. The question everyone asks themselves is, "When should I begin to put together a financial plan to ensure that I have enough funds to comfortably retire?" For me, this question came into focus when I began receiving phone calls from my colleagues, asking me to organize a retirement workshop for principals and vice principals.

I recall meeting Bill McBay back in 2002 when he provided a retirement workshop for the Waterloo Region District School Board (WRDSB). I remembered how much I learned from Bill at that time, so ten years later, I contacted him to provide retirement workshops for our administrators. It has become quite evident how complex retirement planning can be. There are so many questions to consider. When I retire, will I have enough money to travel? Do I still want to work part time after retirement? What do I need to do to get my estate in order? Do I need a will? Should I be an executor to a will? How much money is enough money for retirement? How much money do I need to set aside for my children's post secondary education? Where do I invest my money — annuities, mutual funds, GICs, other? Do I need a financial advisor? What should I look for in finding a competent and professional certified financial advisor?

In his book, *Myths and Truths of Financial Planning Throughout Your Life,* Bill answers these questions and more. The book is easy to read and understand as you navigate the complex world of financial planning. Bill provides many concrete anecdotes to illustrate his points while infusing his subtle sense of humour, which keeps you engaged throughout the book. He skillfully breaks down the many myths about financial planning and provides truth and facts for you to begin to move this topic more to the top of the list of your life's priorities.

Each year for the past five years, Bill has presented retirement workshops to the principals and vice principals of the WRDSB. Much of what he presents in his workshops is reflected in this book. I have received many positive comments about how much people enjoy Bill's knowledge and expertise as well as how he communicates the topics as a workshop presenter. Many administrators attended more than one of his workshops over the years, always walking away with something new that they did not know before. That in itself is a testament to, and reflection of, Bill's more than twenty years expertise in the field of financial planning.

Everyone should read *Myths and Truths of Financial Planning Throughout Your Life* whether they are just beginning to think about about financial planning leading to retirement or whether they already have a plan in place. After reading this book, you will learn how to develop a financial strategy that will lead you comfortably into retirement. Also, you will feel more knowledgeable and confident in taking the next steps in financial planning in order to reach your own goals and dreams.

Helmut Tinnes
Retired Principal
Waterloo Region District School Board

1

THE FIRST BIG MYTH AND THE FIRST GREAT TRUTH

The Big Myth

I can put off planning and do it later — there's no need to do it right away.

The Truth

Life has a crazy way of dealing us the unexpected and then sitting back to watch how we handle it. I believe we need to grow and learn from these challenges, no matter how painful they are. Sometimes it takes a long time — even a lifetime — to answer those big life questions, *Why him? Why me? Why our family?* Etc. etc.

I was told early on in this business to look after the ones I loved first, so my parents were my first clients. When I met with them to discuss their financial plan, they had just gone through a life changing event. The company that was my Dad's employer for many years suddenly closed, leaving them with few options for the last leg of the race to retirement.

Already in his mid-fifties, Dad decided to start a new business, taking on all the challenges that come along with business ownership. Those include not only everything that is required to start and run the business, but the need for a whole new look at financial planning.

At this incredibly busy time in both my parents' lives, I think it was lucky for us that I was also starting a new business in the world of financial planning, and that my parents took the time to support me in my new venture and meet with me to discuss their financial planning. I use the word "lucky" only to point out that in this case, I believe the ***only*** reason why my parents took the time during that very busy portion of their lives, was to help me in my new business. As parents, what we want to do whenever possible is help our children, and my parents were no different. They did help me many times throughout my life and this time, in their minds, was no different.

At the time, we both would have agreed to that statement I'm sure. But in hindsight, it was very different. The fact that I was starting out in this new career and their desire to help me and give me the best support they could, overrode the fact that they were very busy themselves and probably had enough other pressing things to attend to.

I was, quite frankly, in over my head at that early stage in my career, and I definitely didn't want to screw this up for anyone, let alone my parents. Fortunately, my company employs seasoned veterans in the business for just these situations, and with their help we were able to complete the plan that suited my parents' situation. The plan showed some insurance needs and highlighted some work to do to reach Dad's retirement goals after investing in his new venture.

I didn't realize at the time how important it was that I was in this business. Unfortunately, I soon found out.

A short eighteen months after we put the plan in place, I lost my Dad to a massive heart attack. He was only 59, and as far as we all could see had been as healthy as ever. His was the classic case of "never missed a day's work in his life."

As you can imagine, there was much to do, given that they had a new business, new clients, new employees, new vendors and new creditors. Both my Mom and brother worked in the family business, so of course they were left to deal with all the business issues while trying to grieve the loss of husband and father.

As a newer advisor, as you watch money always being paid *to* the insurance company, it's easy to forget why you are paying those premiums. But in fact, it was the planning we had done months before that made it possible for them, as well as me, to concentrate on grieving the loss of my father.

The lessons I learned through that time, and am still learning, have helped me through my career and given me the tools to help others financially during life's most difficult times.

I've often said that financial planning is not something that people decide to do when they wake up one Saturday morning before they head to the farmer's market. In fact, it often falls well below washing their hair on many people's priority lists. I get that.

That may be the reason for Big Myth No. 1: I can put off planning and do it later — there's no reason to do it right away. The Big Truth is: Don't put it off — there's every reason to do it right away.

2

WHAT IS A FINANCIAL PLAN?

People often put off doing a financial plan simply because they think it's a lot of work, and that they'll end up with a 2" thick binder they'll never look at. This may have been true at one time, but it certainly isn't today.

Basically, a financial plan is simply a conversation with your financial advisor, in which you set out what you want to do in your life, how much that will cost and then plan how you will be able to fund it. For example,

- What do you want to do?
- What are you trying to accomplish?
- What keeps you up at night?
- What makes you happy?
- Where do you want to go?
- Where do you want to travel?
- How often do you want to travel?
- How many kids do you want to have?

Your answers to these and many other questions that are

important to you will form the basis of your financial plan. I call this a baseline plan.

Sounds easy, right? Well it can be if you are doing it right, with the right person, at the right time and under the right conditions. It all has to be comfortable, and then it comes together quite nicely.

I like to sit with my clients at my computer and plug in the information they give me about their needs and wants. Although you might think that is the most important part, it's not. It's the conversation we have during that time that is most important.

I send them a list in advance of our meeting of all the things they should bring with them (see below), so they are prepared with wills, bank statements, etc.

Recommended Document List

- ☐ Wills and Power of Attorney documents
- ☐ Mortgage/loan statements
- ☐ Investment statements
- ☐ Pension statements
- ☐ Separation and divorce documentation
- ☐ Prenuptial agreement
- ☐ Incorporation documents
- ☐ Buy/Sell agreements
- ☐ Insurance policy statements
- ☐ Credit card statements
- ☐ Bank statements
- ☐ Tax return documentation
- ☐ Rental property/cottage documents
- ☐ Any documents you may have questions about

I enter their information, hit a button and from that I can tell them whether they are on track to where they want to be, or whether they need a bit of work. Again, it's all pretty easy. I often refer to the Wizard of Oz movie where the Great and Powerful Oz tells us to look away from the man behind the curtain. I feel that by doing plans *with* clients instead of doing plans *for* clients, I don't need to have the curtain up at all. Just an honest conversation and data entry can create a great plan.

We can look at different scenarios, such as early retirement or other options and see what those do to the plan. That's what most people want to know, and that's what this type of financial planning does for them. Questions such as *What if we did this?* or *How does this affect the timeline?* can be answered on the spot if you are working with your advisor to complete the plan.

3

WHEN TO DO A FINANCIAL PLAN

A financial plan is not something you do once and never go back to it. It's not a "set it and forget it" type of thing. It's a living, breathing document that needs to be revisited at times when it is likely to change.

Some appropriate times to consider a new financial plan, or at least a review of the existing one, are:

- Getting married
- Having a child
- Coming into an inheritance
- Winning the lottery
- Getting a big promotion or new job
- Losing your job
- Getting divorced
- Losing a spouse
- Global Pandemic??

Because it's so simple, there's no excuse any more not to do it. After all, isn't your peace of mind worth that brief conversation?

4

HOW TO CHOOSE THE RIGHT FINANCIAL ADVISOR FOR YOU

At many times throughout our lives we need to rely on a friend or an advisor, sometimes the same person. An advisor, by definition, is someone we can trust, lean on and ask for advice in an area in which they have some expertise.

Let's say for example I want to take up fishing, and I have a friend who's known for landing tons of fish for the barbecue all summer long. He could tell me which lake to go to, which fishing hole has the best fish, how to bait the hook, what pole to use, how to hold it, how to jig it — maybe even what the heck jigging is! He might be a great fishing advisor for me — or he might not.

Before following him into the wilderness with my expensive new fishing gear, I'll ask him some questions. For example, I'll ask what makes him such a good fisherman and why he is so successful in catching fish.

If he tells me he read a book last week and has a great new fishing pole and he thought he'd like to tell people about it — maybe I won't listen to him. But maybe he'll tell me he learned to fish as a young child from his dad, who taught him special things you just can't learn from books. If he tells me also that he's so nuts about fishing that he's out there on the water every waking hour, every moment he can — then I can see he understands fishing because he lives it.

That's the guy I want to take me fishing!

The process you follow in finding the right financial advisor for you is much the same — you ask the right questions and listen for the answers. You need to satisfy yourself that this person can give you the advice you need.

Probably the first things to find out about in your initial conversation are the person's education and experience. What designations do they hold? Have they been doing this work for 10 days or 10 years or 30 years?

While they are answering these straightforward questions, pay attention to how they make you feel, because that's a strong indication of whether or not they are right for you. You'll be speaking with this person at some emotionally charged times in your life, so you'll want them to offer comfort and understanding as well as hard core financial advice.

Are they showing an interest in you and your situation, or just expounding on their own brilliant financial expertise?

Do they listen more than they speak? Do they ask questions before giving suggestions? These are signs of a good advisor — after all, how can they give you the right guidance if they don't listen to your story? Should everyone who has given birth to a child, become engaged or lost a loved one be treated in the same way? Not at all. Every one of us is unique, and good advisors understand and work with that fact.

In this initial conversation, if you realize you can exchange information about your feelings and how they affect your financial objectives, and if you can tell them something without thinking twice about it or holding back, then you're probably sitting across from the right advisor for you.

It may take several attempts before you find this person, so here are some guidelines on what to ask and what kind of answers to look for.

What Are Their Qualifications?

As I suggested before, find out about their qualifications right away, which you can easily do by asking what education and designations they have. Ask not only how long they've been working in this field, but whether they've been with the same firm for a long time or worked for shorter periods at various firms.

You might ask, or they might volunteer, why they switched firms. If the advisor is comfortable in their own skin and confident in their abilities, this will feel like a natural conversation and not an interview. Not only will it let you see how comfortable they are in speaking to you, but also give you a feel for how they communicate.

Do they talk down to you and use lots of financial jargon? Not a good sign. Communication is a vital component of a good financial advisor relationship, and this is your first opportunity to see how this person scores on that aspect.

How Do They Get Paid?

It's a good idea to ask them how they get paid, and pay close attention to how comfortable they are in answering and how clear the answer is.

A competent and honest advisor should be happy to tell you how they are compensated. This is, of course, their livelihood so they do expect to earn a living, but it needs to be to your benefit and not at your expense. They should be motivated to help you as well as earn an income for themselves.

I personally make money when my clients make money, and I tell them that. I also tell them that if at any time in our relationship they feel I am not doing right by them, they can and should move on. A relationship by definition is between two people, parties or items.

If, on the other hand, someone starts talking in generalities and never fully explaining how they are paid, you should be wary of this person.

Do They Give You Options?

Here's another big red flag to watch out for — an advisor who wants to lock in your money for any given period, whether it's three years or seven years or more. If you are grieving the loss of a loved one, they may tell you this is in your best interest because you shouldn't have to risk making bad decisions in this emotional time. That's true — but locking your money up is almost always a bad decision!. (Guaranteed investments with ability to withdraw throughout the term would be an exception.)

Locking your money in can mean many different things.

Locking into a Guaranteed investment for a term of five years to get the best rate, well that's just the way it goes. That's how guaranteed investments work. You have an amount to invest and the bank or financial institution sets the rates for different time lines. You can invest for as little as 30 days and in some cases as long as ten years. The average would be five years or under. Traditionally, the longer you lock in your funds the higher the rate of interest you will earn.

If guaranteed investments are what you need to do based on your risk tolerance, then you will have to lock in your money. Depending on your situation, you might feel better locking your investment in for a shorter time or a longer time. It might not have anything to do with the rate.

Sounds crazy doesn't it? Not really. Investing doesn't always have to do with the rate of return. In fact, what I refer to as the soft factors are often even more important.

For example, if you just lost a loved one and you have the proceeds of a life insurance policy you need to invest, you want to make sure you are a good steward of your investments, but your head isn't really in the game right now. You don't want to risk losing any money, so mutual funds probably aren't the way to go. What do you do?

I would suggest shorter term investments of 30 days through to one year. This will get the money working for you but not locked in too long.

Where I have seen issues arise is when advisors attempt to lock funds into mutual funds. Mutual funds should not come with a locked in period. If they do, then they are probably in something called Deferred Sales Charge (DSC) or Low Load (LL) funds. These funds are locked into a multi-year schedule where there is a fee to the investor if they redeem the funds prior to the end of the schedule. The reason for this reducing fee schedule is to ensure the commission paid to the advisor is recouped if the client removes their investment.

When you invest in these types of mutual funds, the advisor receives an upfront commission equal to upwards of 5% of the investment amount. That amount traditionally is not paid back if you pull out. The fee you pay stays with the investment company.

I need to point out, though, that these types of investments are not always bad. When you have, beyond a shadow of a doubt, the timeline to invest without pulling the money and incurring the fee, then they could be used. ***But***, the only reason they would be used instead of the same type of fund that doesn't have the fee associated with it, is the compensation to the advisor.

That's right, there is a version of every mutual fund that has no sales fee associated with it. So, if your advisor is suggesting the one with the upfront compensation, it is important to understand why, and all the risks associated with it before you choose.

Some advisors might suggest that if the money is for longer term investments, such as a pension transfer or RRSP, there is no reason not to use the DSC or LL funds. In fact, I was one of those advisors early in my career. I quickly changed my process after seeing people go through financial difficulty due to job changes, marital breakdown or just bad money choices, and need to pay fees to to access those funds as the money wasn't invested long enough.

So, I guess the moral to this story is, like all of them in this book, understand your options and work with a trusted advisor and you will reduce the chances of paying extra fees or losing out on opportunities because your money is locked in.

You may be having a hard enough time deciding what to wear or what to cook for dinner without having to think about major financial decisions that could have long lasting effects. A good advisor will give you options and explain how they work, including timelines. You need to be sure that if you make a decision on Monday and change your mind on Tuesday, you can do that and it will not incur any costs or reduce your options from that point on.

This way, you can take financial decisions off your to-do

list knowing they are taken care of, and get back to the grieving process.

The same caution about locking in your money also applies whether you've just had a child or are preparing to get married. Always make sure you understand your options — and that you ***have*** options if you change your mind.

Choosing a financial advisor is probably the most important step in the whole process of financial planning. Don't settle for the first person you meet. Seek out qualified people, interview them as I've outlined here, evaluate your options and you'll do fine.

If you don't know where to start in your search, you might check out the website www.fpcanada.ca for a list of Certified Financial Planners in your area. You should also ask your friends and family if they can refer you to someone they trust.

Use some or all of the questions so you can better interview the person who will ultimately have a lifetime relationship with you and your financial future. Hopefully you will end up with an advisor who not only has the technical knowledge, but has your interests at heart and makes you feel comfortable and secure.

A World of Confusion

Just to complicate your search, you need to know that not all advisors are the same. There are a number of similar skills a trusted financial planner must have to be successful in completing plans for you. Skills like big picture thinking, critical thinking, knowledge of tax savings during life and at death, risk management and investment planning, just to name a few. Those, as well as the ability to communicate relevant information in a language that you can understand, are just a few of the important items to consider.

Unfortunately our industry also has many designations, which really don't help clear things up for those who are looking for the right advisor for them. You can deal with a long list of different types of "advisors" but it can be very confusing which educational designations you should look for based on what your needs are.

For that reason, I have compiled a list of some of them, which you will find in Appendix I to this book. Keep in mind that designations, although very important, are still only one part of the big picture in finding your trusted advisor for life. The other pieces are very personal to you and your gut. I hope this list will help you figure out what designations you want your trusted financial planner to have. Each one of those sites will have a list of advisors that carry those designations. Try there and see if you can find some more candidates to interview.

I feel I also need to point out something very important about this process that might be lost, or could be misunderstood, while reading this book.

Many advisors — in fact most of them that I know, including myself — don't start in this business with all the education and designations I am referring to. It took me almost a decade to realize the importance of education in our business. What I mean is, there are good people in our business that might not have their designations yet. They might not show up on a website listing designated advisors or in the Google search for CFP. But they could be great, honest advisors who are working in the best interests of their clients.

You might find out about them from a friend or family member. Get referrals from someone at your work place.

These are still great places to start your search. Remember I said your gut has a lot to do with this process. So knowing they have done well for someone you know is important for sure. Maybe they don't have a designation currently but are working toward it. You will never know unless you meet with them and ask these important questions.

I've often thought that if people invested a similar amount of time finding an advisor as they do choosing the interior options of their next car or decorating ideas for the upcoming renovation, we would all be better off.

Questions for your potential financial planner

This is meant to be only a guideline for questions. Feel free to use as many or as few as you wish. The real benefit will come from the conversation you have with your advisor and how comfortable you feel hearing them answer these questions. That, along with your "gut", will most likely lead to a long lasting and mutually beneficial relationship.

Experience

1. How many years have you been providing financial planning?
2. How many clients do you personally service?
3. Do you have any specialty areas of financial planning? If so, what are they?
4. Have you always worked with this company/firm/partner? If not, can you give me an idea of your career path so far?

Education

1. What professional designations do you hold?
2. Are you working towards any other designations?
3. How do you keep up on the changing financial environment?
4. How many Continuing Education (C.E.) credits do you acquire each year?
5. Where do you get those C.E. Credits?

Personal

1. When do you plan on retiring?
2. What would happen to your clients upon your death? Retirement? Disability?
3. What kind of hobbies do you have? What do you do in your spare time?
4. How are your personal financial planning goals coming along?
5. Why did you get into the field of financial planning?

Service

1. How often do you meet with clients?
2. What can I expect from you at those meetings?
3. How often do you update the engagement letter with clients?
4. What fees do you charge for planning?

5. Do you charge fees to invest through you? If so, could you explain the fees and how they work?
6. Can you give me an example of a time you gave a client excellent service?
7. Can you give me an example of a time you gave a client poor service and what you did to make it right?

5

THE MYTHS ABOUT FINANCIAL PLANNING FOR PEOPLE ABOUT TO BE MARRIED

So you've decided to get married — congratulations! I wish you well as you embark on this wonderful, exciting new stage in your life.

You may feel that financial planning is way down on your list of things to take care of when there are exciting wedding details to look after, but I urge you to take some specific actions along these lines for the sake of your future happiness.

When I was young, I used to be in the wedding industry

and fully understand how much more fun it is to discuss cakes, DJs, flowers and dresses than financial planning. But let me assure you, if you take the financial part of starting your life together seriously, you will be able to enjoy the memories of the amazing day your lives started together for many more years.

There are three Myths that prevent newly engaged couples from taking the steps they should do:

Myth No. 1

People have agreements to protect themselves if they split up. We love each other and we won't be splitting up, so why think about these things?

Myth No. 2

Prenuptial agreements, or what are commonly referred to as Prenups, are for movie stars and the wealthy.

Myth No. 3

We're still young and don't have children yet, so we can put off financial planning till later.

FINANCIAL PLANNING IS NOT about splitting up. It's about improving the quality of your lives together, so let me share with you some truths.

6

THE TRUTH ABOUT FINANCIAL PLANNING FOR PEOPLE ABOUT TO BE MARRIED

If not the number one reason, money is high on the list of reasons marriages break up. Managing money is tough.

It's one thing to meet your soulmate and be thrilled that you love the same theatre or the same food or the same types of vacation. But if one is an over-spender and the other is a tightwad, that's a recipe for disaster — no matter how much you both love Star Trek.

If couples spent as much time planning their finances as

they do planning their wedding, they would be much happier throughout their lives because money would no longer be a cause of friction between them.

When I bring up the subject of a relationship plan, couples usually throw their hands in the air in horror. “Oh no,” they say, “we love each other. We’re never going to part and we trust each other implicitly. We don’t need a prenup. Besides, prenups are for movie stars, not ordinary folks like us.”

OK, there are the myths right out in the open. Now let’s look at the truth.

It’s About More than the Money

When my wife and I started out together, we didn’t do these things I’m advocating now — which is why I know it’s so important. Who knows, maybe I might still be married if we had. Probably not, but it’s the thought that counts!

At the beginning of our marriage, my wife paid all the bills, and it stressed her out. I didn’t have experience paying household bills and I couldn’t really see what the problem was. But the more important question is, why was she paying the bills? And the answer is that she had always done it and she just continued to do it after we were married. We didn’t have any discussion around something as menial as bill paying.

Of course, I just let her do it — it never occurred to me to do otherwise. But before it got to be a problem between us, we sat down and talked about it. I offered to take on the bill paying, which she was happy to give up, and that settled that problem there and then. All it took was the conversation.

OK, so maybe it wasn’t so much a conversation but more the way we came to the end of an argument that started with her asking me, “Why do I have to look after all this?” We would have saved this argument if we had a proper conversation in the first place. Hence this chapter of the book!

So one decision that forms part of the relationship plan, is who is going to do what in your married life.

Separate or Co-mingled, that Is the Question

Should your finances be co-mingled or should you keep things separate? I can't answer that for you, but you need to find an answer that suits you both — that's part of the conversation.

There are several ways to divide your finances.

- All in one pot
- His and hers (or his and his, or hers and hers as the case may be)
- His, hers and theirs

As well as probably many others, but we will concentrate on these main three for now.

If you decide all the money belongs to you both and it is to be looked after jointly, you need to understand what that might mean.

For example, if each partner is reluctant to buy a personal item because they feel guilty using "their" money for their own needs, resentment will soon build.

What happens if the money has always been co-mingled and now one of the partners gets a new job that pays twice as much as the old one. If everything still goes into the same account and becomes "theirs", is that fair?

Sometimes it's better to make the last one on the list, "his, hers and theirs". In this case, an agreed amount of money goes into the joint account each month to pay for the shared expenses. Each partner also has his or her own personal account to be used as they wish.

An example of how this might help things in everyday life could be something as simple as being able to freely comment on a nice new blouse or pair of shoes your spouse is wearing. If that is what they are spending their money on, then you can feel free to give them a compliment without them thinking you are trying to determine the value and whether or not they spent too much on it and a payment for household expenses may get returned due to insufficient funds because of it. A very different response might be received for the same comment.

So really, you could surmise that proper financial planning can lead to more genuine compliments and maybe even more of them. Now you can put an X in the "Financial Planning Makes Everything Better" box. If one actually existed. Oh look, there it is!

All these ideas are simply that — ideas. Ideas that need work to figure out and implement. It can still take some time and conversation to get the balance right, so I recommend you have this conversation together, with the assistance of your advisor. Again, it's part of the relationship plan.

Isn't this Just for the Wealthy?

No, that's another myth. Here's the truth.

The main reason wealthy people have prenuptial agreements probably is to protect their wealth in the event the marriage breaks up. The wealthy tend to think differently from the rest of us, so they probably have no problem with that. It could also be that we hear about them most often in magazines we find in the grocery store checkout. Let's be honest, it seems like some of these stars can't stay married for longer than a haircut lasts, so why not have a good lawyer draft something up!

However, most people I talk to wonder why they should even be thinking of an ending when their lives together are just beginning. The answer to that is that a Relationship Agreement is not just about what happens if there is an end; it's more about what happens during your married life. For example, you should establish the roles and responsibilities of each partner, including but not limited to:

- Who is going to decide how much to spend on Christmas?
- Who is going to shop for the children?
- Who is going to cut the grass, or who is going to pay for the grass to be cut?

- Who is going to clean the house or pay for it to be cleaned?

These, of course, are just examples. You will decide together what you need to outline and agree on — that is the purpose of the conversation.

This process doesn't even have to end with a document at all. It may well be that the conversation itself is enough, so that both of you know where you stand and how you're going to do things.

One item you might decide on — and this is wise — is that if either of you feels the relationship plan is going off track you will immediately sit down and have another conversation to sort it out. Maybe it is a place you will go or a code word you will say to indicate that one needs to start that conversation. It doesn't have to be major things either.

For example, it might be going off track for someone if there isn't enough couple time, too many new purchases or the cable bill is too high. The list is long as well as different for every couple.

It doesn't have to be money driven either. The issue might not start as a financial one, but if there are underlying financial issues that weren't properly discussed, it might end up being about finances. What's that old adage about the root of all evil? Might not be the start of all evil, but could end at the root if you are picking up what I'm throwing down.

Of course, things change in people's lives over the years, and that's why your plan needs to be revisited at all major milestones. This is your relationship plan, and having it in place will provide peace of mind as it adds a level of trust to your lives together.

Can't We Put this Off Until We Have Children?

This is a very naive idea, yet very common. Some parts of financial planning are all about timing. I'm not talking about getting the promotion to manager because no one else would take it and you were standing beside the owner at the time. I'm talking about putting things in place at a time when you can, instead of waiting too long for the time when you can't. Life insurance is one of those products that have a place in most young people's financial plans, but sometimes doesn't get added until it is either too late or too expensive.

Life insurance is meant to replace the income of the insured person, pay any loans that person might have left or their death created, and leave their loved ones with the freedom to take the proper amount of time to grieve their loss.

When young people meet and a relationship starts to flourish, the thought of that relationship ending due to premature death is not often anywhere on the radar. I get that. It's human nature.

But let me ask you a question. What if you could be guaranteed to buy the house of your dreams, send your children to the best university or college and not have to live paycheque-to-paycheque no matter if one of you were taken away? Would you be interested? Well the vehicle to make those things possible already exists: life insurance. But you're young. You don't want to talk about your mortality, do you? Nobody does — and that's the problem.

Somewhere between the day we are born and the day we die, life insurance is taken off the table as an option. Ask someone who has applied for insurance and been told they are not able to get it because of a recent fight with cancer or heart attack; ask them how much they would have bought the day before if they had only known what was coming, and you might have a different view on how it fits into *your* plan. You remember that old song that says, "You don't know what you've got till it's gone"? Well that's life insurance.

If you spend the time to explore your options for life insurance while you're still young and healthy, you'll end up having more money to put towards the more enjoyable parts of financial planning — the saving, buying and paying down parts.

Don't wait till you have debt, children and financial responsibilities to ponder your need for life insurance, look at it as early as you can. Get the *Young and Healthy* discount. The *Pay Less for More* deal or the *Buy it Now and Own it Later* deal. Whatever you want to call it doesn't really matter. But explore it and understand why it is important to your plan, sooner than later.

Financial planning is not about everyone being the same. It is about us all having access to the same products, plans and concepts and using the ones that best fit our own situation. So figure out your situation, the sooner (younger) the better. You'll be happy you did.

The Conversation

I've talked a lot about the conversation that leads to your relationship plan, and you might be wondering where to begin. So I've created the following list of starter questions for you each to consider in advance. Take a look at it together, not to actually discuss it because that should take some forethought, but just to see if there are other items either of you wants to include.

Don't let these questions create an argument. This is not about winners and losers, but about conversation and discussion. If you do it properly in advance, you can avoid argument and resentment in the future.

Also, don't let this be the list you take folded up in your pocket to the first date — unless of course you would like it to be the last date. Just saying...

The Starter List

- How much do you think we should put aside each pay to save for our retirement?
- When do you want to buy a house?
- Are there plans for either of us to go back to school?
- How will we spend our weekends or days off? What kind of expense will that entail?
- How often will we take vacation each year? What would be an excellent vacation and how will we pay for that or save for it?
- What kind of debt do each of us have presently?
- How do you see us paying down that debt when we are together?
- Will we combine our incomes in one joint bank account or keep separate accounts?
- On average, what is the balance of your bank account the day before payday?
- Does paying bills and making financial choices overwhelm you?
- Do you know what your credit score is?
- Have you ever been forced to declare bankruptcy or financial proposal?
- What hobbies do you have and what cost do they carry? How do we plan for those expenses?

- Have you ever completed a budget?
- How are we going to budget?
- Do you use a software program to keep track of what you earn and what you spend?
- Do you pay for things with cash, debit or credit regularly? Why?
- Do you already have a financial planner? Who will we use as a couple?
- Where do you bank? Should we bank at the same institution and if so, which one will we use?
- How long do you see yourself working until you want to retire?
- If you were to lose your job at any point throughout our life together, how do you think you might handle that? What would you expect from me? How could we prepare for that and similar situations now, just in case?
- What about money stresses you out?
- What about money makes you happy?
- What did your parents teach you about money?
- How many credit cards do you have and what are the balances on them right now?

So there's your starter list. Make a date with your partner, chill a bottle of wine or apple juice and have your conversation. With your relationship plan in place, money should never become an issue or an irritant in your lives.

Tip for those who have paid off their homes

People spend many years paying off their mortgages and then get to the end and don't know what to do next. It's like the

dog that chases the car, catches it and doesn't know what to do with it. Now what? Here are a few ideas.

Take a deep breath, relax and congratulate yourself on your accomplishment. Have a ceremonial celebration of burning or shredding the documents that held you to the mortgage for so many years. Raise a glass and toast the next stage of your life. Then, go back to the bank and get a Home Equity Line Of Credit (HELOC) on your home for the maximum amount you can.

Yes, I just said go back into debt — kind of. Here are the reasons for my suggestion so you can better understand why not having a HELOC, could be a bad idea.

1. Fraudsters have learned how to put a mortgage on your home if none exists and rack up a debt that could leave you with a very large mortgage or worse. In some cases, people are being forced out of their homes as the bank comes in and takes the home over in power of sale. All for a mortgage you didn't even put on your property yourself.

The immediate reaction is to get lawyers involved, and that increases your costs with little to no expectation of getting anything back. Regular property and casualty insurance policies on your home do not cover that fraud, and your largest assets could be gone with no recourse. In some cases you might have purchased title insurance that could help, but again all policies are not created equal.

Even if you take my advice, I would look further into what your policy covers and if you have title insurance or not. Keep in mind, you can't sue someone if you don't know who it is, and I'm sure they didn't use their real names on the fraudulent mortgage against your home.

Having a HELOC on your paid-for home is similar to having a flashing light on the dash of your car. Picture a thief with a brick running past cars in a parking lot with those lights, looking for one that doesn't have one before they throw a brick through the window and grab your belongings. Consider a collateral registration with a bank as the same thing as those little flashing lights.

You can't put two *first* mortgages on your property for up to 80% of its value, and the fraudsters know that. So they keep on walking past your home's title until they find someone that owns it outright. I should point out that indeed you can have multiple mortgages on a property, but even the criminals don't want to spend the time to figure out how much the mortgage they would like to put on your home fraudulently can be. Criminals are a lazy bunch in my opinion, which is why they are criminals. They want to find the fully paid-for homes and put a mortgage on them that falls under the radar of everyone, especially the real owners.

2. A line of credit secured against your home will ensure you get the best interest rate you can find in most cases, the exception being when car manufacturers are effectively giving away money with 0% interest. (By the way, if you are offered that on a car purchase, take it. Someone else's money for free is almost always a good idea!) Mortgage companies have become very savvy at creating products to give you the protection I am talking about, as well as the flexibility to use the equity available for many different types of loans, including personal, credit cards, business investments and leveraging if you are so inclined.

3. Another reason is that there may be a time in your life when you are looking for money and you may not want to cash in investments to get access to funds. The market might be down, fees may have you tied in, or you may just not want to slow down the momentum of your investments. Whatever the reason, you have run out of money and you don't want to do a reverse mortgage. (I would suggest that a reverse mortgage should be your last option, if ever.) So having access to cheap funds would be very helpful.

In this current low interest rate environment, having access to funds that could cost you less than you are earning on them in your investments, or in some cases even create a tax deduction for the interest you pay on those funds, is called leveraging. This should be discussed in detail with your advisor before making any decisions in that area. Leveraging adds another level of risk to investing, but it can be worth it if done properly. It is definitely, however, something that needs to be discussed with a competent and trusted financial advisor before you do anything.

So to summarize, not only can you protect yourself against losing it all due to identity theft, you can also ensure you have access to quick, (liquid), low cost, (lower than almost all other debt options) and in some cases, tax deductible funds.

As with everything else in this book, I suggest you seek the help of a qualified professional on the lending options. Mortgage brokers can give you the lay of the land with all mortgage company options instead of asking your bank directly. You should, of course, discuss all aspects with your trusted financial advisor.

7

THE MYTHS ABOUT PROVIDING FOR YOUR CHILD'S FUTURE

You've just brought a new life into the world — how awesome is that? As you gaze at your child in wonder, counting toes and fingers and drooling over that smile (OK, we know it's just gas but we love it anyway!), it's natural that you want to do everything in your power to provide a good life for this new member of your family.

One thing you need to know, however, is that there's a whole industry out there just waiting to take advantage of this desire. Did you notice, for example, in the waiting room or even the delivery room at the hospital there are signs everywhere telling you to "Save for your children's education"? Those signs are often put there by those selling scholarship plans. Those who may want to get you signed up before you have a chance to research the alternatives and choose the best option for you.

There's also a great deal of confusion about the whole question of insurance for children and how it fits in the overall financial picture.

Myth No. 1

You should sign up for a Registered Education Savings Plan (RESP) as soon as your child is born.

Myth No. 2

Buying insurance on a child's life is just plain wrong, because you should never profit financially from the tragedy of a child's death.

Myth No. 3

Putting money in a trust account will ensure the child gets it only when they are able to handle it.

These myths are rooted firmly in the fact that new parents are in a highly emotional state — albeit happy emotions — and it's easy to let those emotions make wrong decisions that will affect your own and your child's future.

8

THE TRUTH ABOUT PROVIDING FOR YOUR CHILD'S FUTURE

Funding their Education

If you buy into a Registered Education Savings Plan, commonly referred to as an RESP, you are usually assuming little David or Samantha will need the money for college around age 18, so you expect to be paying a fixed amount every month until then. That's a very long time. It means that no matter your current financial situation or your future needs, you have to take that RESP amount off the top of your monthly income before you can do anything else.

That can be a hardship for many. A single parent with an average salary, for example, might find it a stretch to put $200 away every month for an RESP and still have money for food and other living expenses.

Or perhaps things look fine right now, but maybe you really want to buy a house and that regular, long-term RESP payment is standing in the way.

The truth is, there are many ways to provide for your child's education that don't always include investing in an RESP at birth. Again, I would like to point out that a properly drafted financial plan will include education funding for your children. It will also outline how that funding will fit with other financial goals set out in your plan. Let me explain.

Look After Yourself First

Let's say you have a house with a mortgage. Instead of putting $200 into an RESP every month, you put it into saving for your retirement through a Registered Retirement Savings Plan (RRSP). This generates a tax saving each year, which you then put towards the outstanding principal of your mortgage, thus reducing your mortgage debt faster.

You can then borrow back that same amount of money you paid down on your principal and invest it. That allows you to use the interest on the loan to reduce your taxable income, which in turn gets you a larger tax refund — assuming you were getting a refund to begin with. The process continues over years with the balance of your debt being reduced and the value of your net worth being increased.

Pause here and re-read the last paragraph as many times as you wish, as there is a lot going on in that one.

I don't want you to take this as advice for you personally at all. In fact, I wanted to make sure it was an overwhelming paragraph simply to illustrate that you have options. Many options. Which ones you choose is completely up to you and your situation, comfort level and abilities.

But assuming the concept outlined in the above paragraph, can you see the potential of repeating this process every year for 18 years? You may have paid off your mortgage, and you will have saved appropriately for your retirement. In other words, you are financially healthy.

Then if 18-year-old Samantha tells you she wants to be a brain surgeon and needs help getting there, you have some options.

If your mortgage is paid off, you can borrow against the asset of your home and use that to put Samantha though school. But perhaps there is an even better alternative assuming you now have your mortgage paid off.

Let's say your mortgage payment has been $1,500 to $2,000 a month and now that cash flow is freed up and available for you to help fund Samantha's education. You could choose to use all of the former mortgage payment, or even just $1,500. It won't feel like a hardship for you, because you have been paying it out every month for your mortgage all these years, which is very different from struggling to put away a measly $200 every month at a time when you were not as financially comfortable as you are today.

Not everyone can do as I have suggested, nor should they. But everyone should know there are options available — options you may not know about if you are not working with a financial planner.

I should also point out that if you are not working with a qualified financial planner, these concepts come with an added level of risk that doesn't exist with the proper guidance. A concept alone doesn't have emotions, or preconceived thoughts about money management, but you do. That is the reason the advisor can help ensure the concept you are considering fits ***you*** and ***your*** financial goals.

Tax Refunds Are NOT All Created Equal

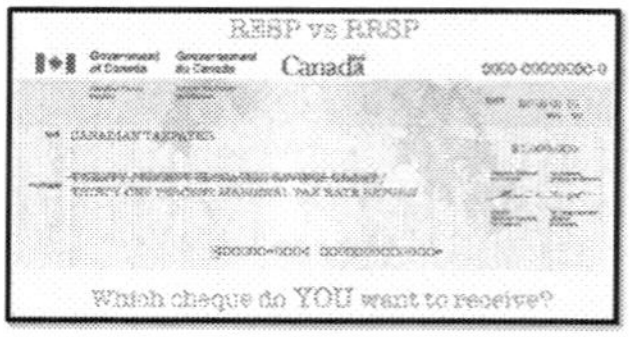

To best understand what I mean, try to picture a very large bank account owned and operated by the Government. (Not operated very well in most cases I should point out, and I am sure you can find many other books about that topic.) All funds from taxes of all different types flow in, and all the payments to Canadians for things like the Canada Child Benefit (CCB)[1], Canadian Education Savings Grant[2] and normal tax refunds, to name just a few, come out of this account.

The revenue of the government is made up of multiple types of tax revenue and profit from government owned Crown Corporations. Therefore it is not a stretch to say that any money that comes to you from the government is a form of tax refund — taxes that you and I have paid at one place or point in our lives.

Based on that analogy, wouldn't it make sense to do what it takes to maximize the amount of money that comes to you from the government? In order to get your fair share, you need to understand what determines the size of the cheque you will get back. In almost every situation the determining factor is your income, which is used to determine your marginal tax rate.

If it is too low, you will be able to take advantage of programs/tax refunds like Canada Learning Bond[3] for RESPs or the Guaranteed Income Supplement[4] if you are retired.

If you have a larger income and pay tax at a higher level, you will receive tax refunds based on interest costs you incurred to invest as well as RRSP deductions that entitle you to a larger refund. Let's use RESP vs RRSP as an example to help you better understand.

An RESP gives you a "tax refund" or Canadian Education Savings Grant (CESG) of 20%, but if you earn more than $44,741 a year you can put the same amount into an RRSP and get a 24.15% tax refund. In either case you are getting money from the government, which is already your money. So wouldn't you rather get 24.15% instead of 20%? It all comes from more or less the same bank account. The top left corner of the cheque still shows a Canadian flag, that's all I'm saying.

The story gets even better, or worse depending on which way you are looking at things, if you have a higher income. The tax brackets in Canada are based on a "more you make, the more we take" philosophy. So, as your income increases, the income earned in each bracket is taxed at a higher rate. For example, if you earn over $48,536 but less then $78,786 and live in Ontario in 2020, you will pay 29.65% of the income earned between those amounts. If you apply that to the RESP discussion we have been having, you are now getting even more back using the same amount of money.

I feel I should also point out that low income earners have the potential to earn even a higher government grant and might even qualify for an education bond as well. So those are also factors to consider when deciding what to invest in. Hopefully by now, you are picking up on the fact that there isn't just one rule for everyone. Financial planning is very personal, and different people can achieve the same results doing things very differently. It's always advisable to seek out the advice of a trained and trusted advisor.

Besides the rate, there is a difference in what you can do with your tax refund under these two plans. When the government issues you a cheque under an RESP, you'd better use it for school or you'll lose it.

In order to get the most out of this type of investment vehicle, how you withdraw funds from the RESP is just as important as how you deposit funds. [5]

The money you get from your RRSP, on the other hand, is yours to spend or use as you wish; a winter holiday in the sun or pay down your mortgage — up to you. If you decide on the mortgage reduction route, this can form an integral part of your lifetime financial plan, including assisting your children with their education.

Although it could be scary to have your children come to you and tell you they were accepted to Harvard, it might also be quite scary having maxed out all the CESG and having them tell you they really just want to draw with chalk on sidewalks for money. (No disrespect to that occupation at all. I love a good chalk covered sidewalk.)

But let's just say you might not be able to get back all the funds you received from the government and the growth on those funds. You certainly won't be able to get back the interest you were charged for your mortgage over those years when you paid the minimum so that you could put money away for your children's education. Even at today's low interest rates, paying lump sums towards your principal can save you tremendous amounts of money and time over a traditional 25 year mortgage.

In other words, look after your own financial situation first, and you will be in a much better position to look after your children's financial needs when the time comes, no matter what those needs are. Good sidewalk chalk is not cheap!

Although I have spent a lot of time suggesting that you might not want to use a RESP to fund your children's or grandchildren's education, there are some situations where it does make sense. If you have been maxing out your RRSP contribution room every year and taking advantage of all the prepayment options on your mortgage, or don't have a mortgage at all, then you are in an ideal position to take advantage of the RESP and Government grant money that comes along with it.

In other words, if you are doing everything else properly and find yourself with extra money that you can focus on education, then why not? Start an RESP and take advantage of the grant, but at least after reading this book, you might not just throw all the money into it without first thinking about all the ways you may or may not be able to get the funds out if the person you are saving for decides not to go to post-secondary school. I feel my job would be complete if you took that extra time to consider the pros and cons of investing for education, instead of just doing it because you picked up a brochure in the hospital maternity waiting room.

The world is always changing

I feel I need to share a story that happens more now than ever before.

Parents start to save for their children's education hoping they will save enough. The children get to the time they need to go to school and find out that even the traditional degree programs now come with co-op options and they have saved too much. Saving too much seems like an oxymoron doesn't it? Well in this case, it isn't. It could mean that a portion of the money redeemed from the RESP will be taxed much higher than intended, as it will be added to the student's income from the co-op placement.

Not all programs have co-op. Not all co-op placements pay their students. But some do and some are very decent incomes when you consider an engineering or similar program.

The last thing I want people to do after reading this book is to use it as an excuse or guide. I certainly don't ever want to hear someone say, "You should never have RESPs or save for education for your children!". That is not what I am saying. I bring this and other ideas and stories to your attention to drive home the fact that everyone needs to plan, and they should do it with a professional trusted advisor. It's a *minefield* of good and bad financial choices out there. Do what you can to ensure you get through life without stepping on any mines, while enjoying the journey at the same time.

Types of RESP

Let's assume for a moment that you have your financial plan in place and decide you do want to invest in an RESP. Not to be a broken record, but I want to point out that I'm not saying RESPs are a bad thing. Not at all. It's just that they are misunderstood and not necessarily used properly by all and right for every situation.

So assuming you have them on your list, you have another decision to make, because there are two types of RESP. One is a scholarship type, and the other is a "save-yourself-and-get-the-grant" type, for lack of a better name. Traditionally, this second type of RESP is invested in mutual funds or investments chosen by the subscriber, aka client, with the help of a financial planner licensed to discuss mutual funds and the other investments available to them.

Scholarship plans are managed by investment companies, and returns can be very good. They are often referred to as "pooled funds", as all the people that invest in these accounts pool their funds to eventually fund the education of those who have paid into the scholarship. So if you are in a position to comfortably commit to this monthly payment for a long time, then you could reap some substantial rewards.

However, if you have high expenses already for your children (such as hockey, baseball, dance class, to name just a few) and you are relying on your own parents to chip in a few hundred dollars every year for birthdays that could go towards education, it will probably cause you hardship to go the scholarship route. Those payments are considered a premium, and if you default there could be fees and cancellation charges that can become quite expensive. Those fees, or a portion thereof in some cases, become part of the overall return of the pool of funds.

So in summary, those who can afford to go into a pooled fund and stay the course will find themselves doing well when Junior wants to go to school. But in a case where regular ongoing cash flow towards an education plan might be interrupted at some time in the future, the individually invested, personally managed RESP is a better choice. No matter your choice, the funds you put aside for your children's education are exactly that. Keep this in mind so that you don't effectively "over save". Any money that is "over saved" could have been better used in your financial plan in almost every situation.

That being said, please refer to the beginning of this chapter on where education planning fits into a financial plan. You might determine that it doesn't fit in at all, or at least not in the traditional fashion we have come to understand.

Life Insurance on Your Child's Life

The last thing you want to ever go through is the loss of a child, and you certainly are not thinking about that possibility when your child is born. But I'd like you to step back for a moment and look at this in a different light. Here are three stories that may help you understand what I mean.

Bob and Maria

When little Tony was born, Bob and Maria were full of happiness and hope for their new little family unit. Tony was healthy and bright and showed every sign of intelligence. Everyone was happy and relieved. All went well until he was 12.

Then, seemingly out of the blue, their beloved Tony became ill and was diagnosed with a fast-moving form of cancer. Despite the heroic efforts of doctors, within three months Tony passed away.

To say Bob and Maria were devastated is an understatement. Bob managed to hold it together, but Maria couldn't. She went into clinical depression and couldn't work, with no indication as to when she would improve.

This was a dual income family, so to add to the emotional loss of their child, they now had to contend with the financial stress of losing a large part of their income. Bob's own health was also now put at risk.

Both the immediate and long-term effects on their lives were incalculable.

If only they had taken out insurance on Tony's life, the benefit would have helped deal with the financial issues and leave them free to grieve their loss together.

Mike and Lynda

Mike and Lynda were over the moon when Andrea was born. This beautiful, smiling little girl brought more joy to their lives than they could ever have expected.

When their financial advisor suggested they take out a life insurance policy on Andrea's life, their first reaction was negative. First, they didn't want to consider the possibility of Andrea's death, and if that tragedy ever actually took place they certainly didn't want to benefit financially from it. Fortunately, their advisor was understanding, and patiently explained the other side of the picture.

Mike and Lynda took out a limited payment type policy for twenty years, at which time the premiums would stop and the policy would become an asset for Andrea.

The cost of life insurance is based on age, so you can never buy a cheaper insurance policy than one that's purchased at time of birth or a month old. So Mike and Lynda's premium expenses were minimal.

Happily, Andrea thrived, and when she was 23, she announced her plans to marry Ivan. With the insurance in place on Andrea already paid up as an asset, that was one less cost they had to worry about starting out together.

Although in some cases money can be taken from the policy to fund weddings and education, etc., I would like to suggest that it is *not* why you would buy insurance. Any type of insurance that has savings in it should keep that money inside it. Either it is there to offset future increases in the cost of insurance or it is available only on cancelation of the policy. In some cases, however, it can be used as collateral to borrow against in order to get access to that value. A professional, licensed Advisor will explain all options in detail, of course.

Unfortunately, the "savings" part of insurance has been the reason that some policies have been sold improperly instead of purchased to cover a need, now and in the future. So understand why you might consider insurance on your child and work with your trusted advisor to consider your options to ensure you are getting the plan that's right for you.

Steve and Nicole

When Nicole gave birth to little Steve Jr., both Steve and Nicole knew their life was changed forever. But like anyone else, they had no idea what that actually meant.

They purchased some life insurance at the advice of their trusted advisor that not only insured Steve Jr., created cash value in the future and became paid up at a predetermined time in the future, but it also had something called a Guaranteed Insurability Option rider on it. Guaranteed Insurability Option, or GIO as it is often called, is an option to buy insurance in the future without having to provide medical evidence.

No one could even conceive the idea at that time that Steve Jr. would be diagnosed with juvenile diabetes at age 12. But he was.

Because of the GIO rider on the policy Steve and Nicole purchased for him, Steve Jr.'s ability to purchase insurance in the future was not affected by this recent diagnosis. You see, someone with a Type 1 Diabetes is most often not able to get life insurance, and if they are, the rates are very high and the product features very limited. Steve Jr. doesn't have to worry about that. With the policy he has, he will be able to purchase an additional $150,000 of insurance if he wants or needs it, every five years from age 16 to 45. No questions asked. Steve and Nicole's purchase of life insurance guaranteed his health for most of his life.

Remember what I said earlier in the book about asking someone who couldn't get insurance how much they would have bought if they could go back to the day before they were uninsurable? Well you can imagine how relieved Steve and Nicole were once this was explained to them after sharing the news of Steve Jr.'s diagnosis with their advisor.

Trust Accounts

The myth of the trust account stems from its name. People see the word "trust" and they think it's the same as a legal trust, which can specify the age the beneficiary must be before he or she can claim it and for what reason it may be claimed, etc.

With an "in trust for" investment account, however, the age of access is whatever the age of majority is in that jurisdiction. That's it, no matter how immature, financially incompetent or just naive the child may be.

Like other teenagers, little Johnny wants to be popular, and what could be more likely to do that for him than to have lots of money to splash around on his friends? So the moment he reaches the age of majority, whatever may be, off he goes to the financial planner and demands access to his money.

It's important to understand that the planner has no alternative but to give it to him. Not only that, but he can't even call Johnny's parents to let them know what is happening. The words "in trust for" in this case have more to do with the ability for a minor to have access to certain investment vehicles that are not available to them than it is for someone to plan future gifts to them at certain times and after certain milestones in their life.

These types of accounts can also create some additional problems at the death of the settlor, or person who invested the money for the minor, that might not have existed if that type of account wasn't used.

The taxation of these accounts can also vary. The reasons they vary often go unnoticed by those who own the accounts. By that I mean, if the informal or "In Trust Account" is set up with the money going into the account and never coming out to the parent or grandparent who made the deposit, (aka settlor) the income or interest should be attributed to the minor listed in the account.

However, if there had been a withdrawal during the time the minor was still a minor, that would put the trust off side and the income would then be attributed back to the parent or grandparent making the original deposit.

Confusing, right? There are many other instances that need to be properly understood when using these accounts, and I would suggest that your financial planner should go into more detail with you when considering these accounts as a tool in your financial planning toolbox.

So if you should decide to put money in a trust account to save for your child, make sure it is right for you and is done the right way. It should be based on what you decide you want the money for and personally speaking, you might want to make sure you ***don't*** tell the kids about it in advance! (Again, just throwing it out there.)

Critical Illness Insurance on Your Child's Life

The last two words I want anyone to think as they read this book are "insurance poor". Yes, there are many options to insure almost anything, and I'm not suggesting that everyone needs every type of coverage. Not at all, in fact. I am, however, suggesting that you put on or off your list of things to do, the coverages that make the most sense to you. Consider your situation after discussing the subject in detail with your trusted advisor.

Critical illness insurance is quite an incredible product. It pays a lump sum of cash, tax free in most cases, to someone who survives any of the listed illnesses on the policy they purchased. There are as many different types of coverage available as there are types of critical illness for you to get and survive.

Although a relatively new product, it has already gone through numerous increases in cost, product offerings and underwriting requirements. As experience with the claims of this type of product grows, insurance companies are asking for more details and charging more for the risk. What that means to the rest of us is, get it young when you are healthy and when you — or more likely your parents — can afford it.

The insurance companies have even gone as far as creating a product that will pay back to the owner of the policy anywhere from 75% up to 100% of the premiums paid at a certain age. The percentage of premium refund is all dependent on the insurance company, the age of the insured and when the policy was acquired.

So this *is* an example of a policy that can be purchased to cover a risk while at the same time have a backup savings component to it. Of course it should be purchased along with the advice of your trusted advisor. Do you see a pattern forming here? Just checking.

Coercive Tied Selling

As we've been looking at various financial arrangements you need to set up in providing for your child's future — and in fact for other aspects of your financial planning — this seems like a good time to warn you about a myth you may find alive and well and living at your bank. It's called Coercive Tied Selling.

The Myth

You have to hold all your investments with the bank in order to get your mortgage approved.

The Truth

No, you don't. That simple. This information is just plain wrong.

I'm not suggesting that the banks are doing unlawful things and everyone at a bank is breaking the law. Not at all. In fact, the majority of those I have dealt with and continue to deal with are excellent at their jobs and work in the best interest of their clients. The way it should be.

What I am suggesting is that *sometimes*, *some* people at *some* branches of *some* banks have said things that might make clients believe they have no choice but to hold their other investments with them to get a mortgage — or a mortgage with them to get a credit card, or another product to get a different one. This is called "coercive tied selling" and it is against the law. In fact, it is clearly listed on all the major banks' websites, and I have even caught myself reading the brochure while waiting in line to do my own banking.

So why the big warning then? Do you remember the telephone game? The one you played sitting around the campfire, where you start with a phrase or word and whisper it into the ear of the person sitting beside you? Inevitably, by the time you heard what the word or phrase had evolved to on the other end, you wondered if everyone was asleep during the exchange or if they were just trying to mix it up for fun. I am going to suggest that other than the "mix it up for fun" part, some of what people think is coercive tied selling might actually be preferential pricing or bundling of products — both of which are perfectly legal. Here, I'm following what my Mom always taught me and giving everyone the benefit of the doubt.

I'm sure there have been times when someone at a bank has said something like, "If we were to transfer your mutual funds here to the bank, we could get you a better deal." The person hearing that explained to a friend on the way home that they needed to transfer their mutual funds in order to get a mortgage. Period. The telephone game. One or two different or fewer words and the entire context has changed.

That is why you need to be informed and to listen closely. It is also another reason why it is so important to have a trusted financial planner to work with you every step of the way.

The banks certainly make the information about tied selling and what is right and what is wrong available for those who want it. But then again, I know the information is available for me to be a yoga instructor, but I haven't sought it out and read it. (I do have a yoga mat though. Step one in a multi-step program.)

So my purpose with this section is to lead readers interested in understanding more about coercive tied selling and how it works to the website of the bank they deal with to further understand how it might affect them — or simply to be better informed.

There can be some confusion around the act of coercive tied selling and bundling of products or even preferential pricing. The latter two are legal and common practice at businesses everywhere, financial or otherwise. My hope is that this might help to explain the differences so that you will be better equipped to listen for the language used by your bank and determine what they are actually discussing.

Like the rest of this book, I share this information to help you protect yourself from those not working in your best interest. I hope you never have to worry about this, but I want you to understand when it is happening. For that reason, I have taken the following directly from the website of one of the big banks in Canada. This is an example of how the banks are doing a good job of explaining this to their customers by creating brochures and adding to their websites. This is just an attempt to put it all in one place.

From the website

The Bank Act requires banks to inform customers in plain language that Coercive Tied Selling is illegal. ***What is Coercive Tied Selling?***

Coercive Tied Selling is illegal and is prohibited under Section 459.1 of the Bank Act. More specifically, it is against the law for a bank to "impose undue pressure on, or coerce, a person to obtain a product or service from a particular person, including the bank and any of its affiliates, as a condition for obtaining another product or service from the bank". You cannot be unduly pressured to buy a product or service that you don't want from a bank or one of its affiliates, to obtain another bank product or service.

The following two examples will help you understand Coercive Tied Selling and what is not allowed.

1) Your bank's mortgage specialist tells you that you qualify for a home mortgage. However, you are also told that the bank will approve your mortgage only if you transfer your investments to the bank or its affiliates. You want the mortgage, but you do not want to move your investments.

2) You are advised that you qualify for a Registered Retirement Savings Plan (RRSP) loan. However, you are also told that the bank will approve the loan only if you use the money to buy the bank's mutual funds. You want the loan, but you want to invest the money elsewhere.

Both of the above practices are against the law. If you qualify for a product, a banking representative is not allowed to unduly pressure you into buying an unwanted product or service as a condition of obtaining the product you want.

What is not Coercive Tied Selling?

Most businesses look for tangible ways to show their interest in your business and appreciation for your loyalty. Sales practices, such as preferential pricing and bundling of products and services, offer potential and existing customers better prices or more favourable terms. These practices should not be confused with coercive tied selling, as defined by the Bank Act. Many of these practices will be familiar to you in your dealings with other businesses.

Preferential Pricing

Preferential pricing means offering customers a better price or rate on all or part of their business. For example, a printer offers a lower price for each business card if you buy a thousand cards instead of a hundred. A shoe store may offer a second pair of shoes at half price.

Similarly, a bank may be able to offer you preferential pricing – a higher interest rate on investments or a lower interest rate on loans – if you use more of its products or services.

The following two examples will help you understand preferential pricing in banks.

1) After approving your application for a home mortgage, your bank's mortgage specialist tells you that this mortgage would be available at a lower interest rate if you transferred your investments to the bank or its affiliates.

2) After approving your application for an RRSP loan, you are offered a lower interest rate if you use the loan to buy the bank's mutual funds.

The above practices are acceptable. The approval of your mortgage and RRSP loan is not conditional on your taking another bank product or service. Rather you are offered preferential pricing to encourage you to give the bank more business.

Bundling of Products and Services

Products or services are often combined to give consumers better prices, incentives or more favourable terms. By linking or bundling their products or services, businesses are often able to offer them to you at a lower combined price than if you bought each product on its own. For example, a fast-food chain advertises a meal combination that includes a hamburger, fries and a drink. The overall price is lower than if you bought the three items separately.

Similarly, banks may offer you bundled financial services or products so that you can take advantage of package prices that are less than the sum of the individual items.

The following example will help you understand the bundling of bank products and services.

You plan to open a bank account that charges you for individual transactions. You are offered a package of services that includes a comparable bank account, a credit card with no annual fee and a discount on purchasing traveller's cheques. The total price for the package is less than if you purchased each part of the package separately.

Bundling products in this way is permitted because you have the choice of buying the items individually or in a package.

If you can remember a time where you experienced Coercive Tied Selling at a bank or financial institution, you should contact the branch manager of that institution.

You can also contact the Financial Consumer Agency of Canada (FCAC) with a regulatory complaint in writing at:

Financial Consumer Agency of Canada
6th Floor, Enterprise Building
427 Laurier Ave. West
Ottawa, Ontario
K1R 1B9

---

1. https://www.canada.ca/en/revenue-agency/services/child-family-benefits/canada-child-benefit-overview.html
2. https://www.canada.ca/en/services/benefits/education/education-savings/savings-grant.html
3. https://www.canada.ca/en/employment-social-development/services/learning-bond.html
4. https://www.canada.ca/en/services/benefits/publicpensions/cpp/old-age-security/guaranteed-income-supplement/eligibility.html
5. https://www.canada.ca/en/revenue-agency/services/tax/individuals/topics/registered-education-savings-plans-resps/payments-resp/educational-assistance-payments-eaps.html

9

THE BIG MYTH ABOUT PREPARING FOR THE END OF YOUR LIFE

Too many of us don't make appropriate preparation for the end of our lives, because we don't really want to think about it. I've even heard people say they are afraid that if they start planning for their death they may hurry it along! Obviously, that's not true at all, but we human beings can be remarkably superstitious about death and baseball. OK, so I'm a baseball fan. Moving right along...

But preparing for your death is not really about you; it's about your loved ones, those you'll be leaving behind. If you want to make things as easy for them as possible, you will prepare in advance.

As with other stages in life, there are some myths around this preparation that need to be put to rest.

The Big Myth

If you grant someone power of attorney, there will be no problem managing your affairs when you are gone. (First of all, powers of attorney are for when you are alive, executors are for when you are gone.)

10

THE TRUTH ABOUT PREPARING FOR THE END OF YOUR LIFE

Your Estate Plan

You need an estate plan. If both you and your spouse are still living, you should get it in place now. If you have lost your life partner or don't have one at all, it's even more important that you get an estate plan now. It saves huge complications for your loved ones at the time of your death.

The truth is you can create a "simple" estate plan for a living person who still has legal capacity or the ability to make decisions, in an hour or so, but if I'm dealing with the executor of someone who has died, that's a whole other story and it's much more complicated.

Let's say you want to change the beneficiaries of your investments or your life insurance policy. You just tell your advisor what you want, sign the form and it's done. Simple. Or if you want to move your money out of a volatile market, again you just advise your planner and it gets done.

But let's say the person holding your power of attorney (POA) wants to do what's best and reduce your risk by taking you out of the market. By doing this, they may well be protecting your money against market risk but in turn creating an estate risk because it has to go through the estate. You see a POA, although they act as if they are a clone of you, can only do certain things. The one very important thing they cannot do is change or appoint beneficiaries on any asset or change your will. This of course is for your protection, but can lead to some difficult situations if not understood by both your planner and your POA. If any new accounts are opened or certain changes made, your estate will become the default beneficiary on those accounts they make changes to while acting as your POA.

Depending on whether or not you have a will, this could really create a domino effect of other issues that no one would wish upon their worst enemy. For example, it could extend the time it takes to settle your estate, create unwanted legal fees and taxes just to name a few.

This could all be avoided if you put a proper estate plan into place while you are still in the land of the living and understanding.

An estate plan can be very complicated or incredibly simple. The differentiating factors are you and your "stuff". If you want to make a number of specified gifts and bequests based on milestones and achievements, it could be very complicated. But if you want to give everything to a couple of people or places with no strings attached, then it could be quite simple and straightforward. Sometimes simply owning the right type of asset can create a very simple estate plan. One way to cover a number of issues that could come up in an estate that was not properly planned for is to use Accumulation Annuities, (AA's). I call that the AA estate plan.

Why is the AA Estate Plan so important?

An AA, or Accumulation Annuity, can ensure the investment portion of your estate gets to those you wish to receive your assets without a whole lot of time, additional taxes and administration. A properly prepared plan will always address those items and this one is no different.

It serves as a back-up plan to a properly laid out estate plan using wills, trusts and insurance products.

What is an Accumulation Annuity? Great question actually. Quick answer is that they are the best kept secret that insurance companies have been providing for over a hundred and fifty years. They are guaranteed investment products very similar to Guaranteed Investment Certificates or GICs that are found in banks and trust companies all over the globe.

Basically, an AA is a GIC that is sold through insurance companies and falls under the Insurance Act instead of the Bank Act. There are, however, two distinct differences between the AA and the GIC that make them incredible for estate planning. (Check the illustration later in the book for some more differences.)

The first and main difference is the ability to assign a beneficiary to an AA for non-registered money. This is important because a named beneficiary on non-registered money could save the estate thousands in probate tax and legal fees.

The second difference is that they are all redeemable at any time throughout the duration of the invested term. For example, if someone invests in a GIC for five years at 2% and then requires access to the funds before the term is up, they would have to either sell the GIC on the open market, which not all institutions actually allow, or they sit and wait for five years. An AA, on the other hand, can be redeemed at any time for a market value adjustment or MVA. The MVA can be either positive or negative, depending on interest rate fluctuations.

Both of these benefits make them a very attractive investment vehicle for proceeds from a life insurance policy or the sale of the family home. The ability to earn some interest, add beneficiaries and not be forced to make any big financial choices after losing a loved one, not only reduces stress but also saves probate and legal fees if something were to happen to you before you get a chance to start making larger financial plans.

The state of mind you are in while making major financial plans is a very important consideration. Having the ability to effectively buy some time using AAs makes a lot of sense at a few different times throughout your life. I guess it is fair to say that "buying time" is yet another benefit of the AA.

Now back to the AA estate plan. One of the main challenges a POA faces is making changes to investments without the beneficiaries of those investments being changed to the default of estate. A POA can set up a new Accumulation Annuity or investment vehicle that could be used to reduce the risk of their assets, but unless it was properly planned ahead of time, the beneficiary will be the estate, creating a new risk: taxes, time and administration fees.

The AA estate plan suggests that prior to the need for a POA, people open AA accounts for each of the registrations they will ultimately require, e.g. RSP, LIRA, TFSA and OPEN (non-registered).

Once opened, the minimum deposit to keep them active should be made or transferred into these accounts. Depending on the company, that amount could be anywhere from $50 to $1,000 per account. This money sits inside the AA and is earning interest and waiting to become one of the most important parts of the plan.

The next and final step to this plan is to appoint the proper beneficiaries to those accounts, making sure to also appoint secondary or contingent beneficiaries. This is the key to the plan — the secondary beneficiaries.

As these accounts sit there and earn a slight amount of interest (guaranteed products are based on interest rates which have recently been at historically low rates) they will be ready for the POA to use to transfer other assets into without the worry of upsetting the beneficiaries or worse yet, creating unwanted tax and legal fees.

The cost for this plan is quite low: time that you invest in the paperwork to open the accounts and set up the beneficiaries, and the difference between what the minimum in each account will earn based on low interest rates versus other market based investment options. All in all, pretty inexpensive when you consider the savings.

Terminal Illness Benefit

Every life insurance policy in Canada has a built-in contractual right that allows the policy owner access to 50% of the death benefit or face value of the policy once diagnosed with a terminal illness. A terminal illness is defined as an illness that reduces your life expectancy to less than two years. (This should not be confused with Critical Illness insurance.)

This payment is made as a loan against the death benefit, and interest starts to accrue as soon as the cheque is issued. Upon the death of the life insured, the remainder of the death benefit less accrued interest on the loan will be paid to the beneficiaries.

This prepayment of the life insurance can be used for anything or nothing. You may choose to get the best medical care available, or maybe to take the family to Disney. The choice is yours. Either way, it is available and should be discussed as an option whether you decide to use it or not.

Like any other insurance, you hope you will never need it. However, it's a good idea to talk to your planner in advance so that you can make an informed decision if and when the time does come.

11

THE MYTHS ABOUT DEALING WITH THE DEATH OF A LOVED ONE

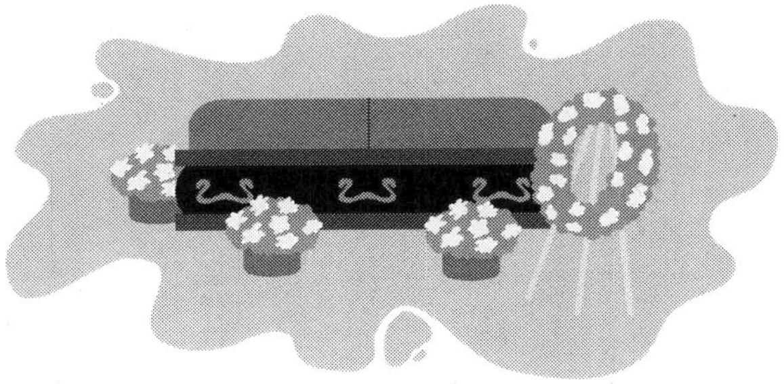

Losing a loved one, particularly a spouse or life partner, is one of the most difficult hurdles life presents us with. Unfortunately, there are a couple of myths that make it even more difficult and could even compound financial difficulties that it may cause.

Myth No. 1

Financial decisions should be made as quickly as possible.

Myth No. 2

When you receive a cheque from the insurance company, you should put it in a GIC or other investment so that it will grow.

12

THE TRUTH ABOUT DEALING WITH THE DEATH OF A LOVED ONE

The truth is, there are some things that should be dealt with as soon as possible, and others than can and should be left until you are in a better emotional condition to consider them carefully. Don't put yourself under extra pressure by trying to do everything while your mind is in a fog.

What to Do Right Away

The first thing to take care of is the wrapping up of the estate if you are the executor. If you are the sole beneficiary of the estate as well as the executor, you have just been given some time. You will not have to rush through anything.

That being said, if you are an executor and there are other beneficiaries, you will want to ensure all the assets of the estate are safe and sound and still earning a regular amount of interest before you can relax totally. The responsibility of those assets until they are distributed, and quite frankly the results of what the executor did while under their control, stays with them for a lifetime afterwards. Executors, or trustees as they are sometimes called, carry ***Lifetime Unlimited Liability.***

In this book we will discuss the situation in which you are the executor and the beneficiary. That is where proper financial planning is required for the next stage. (Stay tuned for an entire book on the duties of an executor, as that job is a busy one if you are doing it for someone other than only yourself.)

If you have recently lost your spouse, I want you to understand that you have one of the most powerful tax deferral options available to you. It is called the spousal rollover. In your time of mourning and loss, may this be the one bright spot, as I know there are few, if any, during that difficult time.

This is the one time you can almost see the faces on the auditors at CRA cringe when you elect the spousal rollover. The rollover allows a spouse to continue to defer taxes on things like joint assets, RSP/RIF redemptions, TFSA accounts. Funds roll over to spouses without triggering any taxes. In the case of the TFSA where no taxes were ever required to be paid, it's the contribution room that rolls over to the spouse.

Although it sounds like a wonderful way to avoid taxes, you may also choose not to use it. This is something that might come up if you have some previous losses to use or a lower income. No matter the reason, this is always a good time to speak with a trusted financial advisor to determine the best route of action for you. As always, I need to point out that tax regimes change over time and are based on where the tax payer resides, so make sure your advisor understands what pertains to you.

This is exactly the time in your life I have been referring to when having a trusted financial advisor is most important. For those who are in that situation and only then starting to realize its importance, it can be quite stressful to start the search then. Please refer to the first chapter where I explain the importance of choosing a financial advisor you can deal with for your lifetime.

The next item is something that, if done right, can make everything else simple in the future. It is the secret the banks won't tell you. In fact, they have created their own workarounds that in some cases put clients and their assets at even greater risk. Try not to be too hard on the banks, as they don't have any other options. They are legislated through the *Bank Act*, and those are the rules they must play within.

The great thing about what I am going to tell you is that it is legislated through the *Insurance Act*. It's how you handle the cheque from the insurance company, and in fact any other money you want to protect for yourself and your own beneficiaries. It's the one secret that could save so much time and money when you are no longer with us — we could have lawyers picketing out front of our offices because of it. OK, that might be a stretch, but the banks certainly wouldn't be happy. It's called the ***Accumulation Annuity*** **(AA)**. You have heard me talk about it in a previous chapter, and here are some more ways to make this your new BFFL (best friends for life). Actually, let me rephrase that, BFFLAB (best friends for life and beyond). Let me explain.

GIC vs AA

Most adult Canadians know what a GIC, or Guaranteed Interest Certificate, is, but many are not familiar with a little gem called an Accumulation Annuity, or AA. First, let me show you the difference between the two, and then I'll explain why and how you should be using an AA.

The actions you take now should be with a view to keeping

or putting your own financial house in order, as well as putting things into place before your own death. In other words, you are looking after yourself in your lifetime, and making things as easy as possible for those you leave behind.

GIC	AA
Guaranteed Interest Certificate falls under bank act.	Accumulation Annuity falls under the insurance act.
Insured under the C.D.I.C (Canadian Deposit Insurance Corporation) $100,000 Per account type and ownership structure. Visit cdic.ca for more detailed information.	Insured by not for profit Insurance company that insures the insurance companies called Assuris. Same basic limits of coverage as CDIC. Visit assuris.ca for more detailed information.
Non Registered accounts can NOT have a beneficiary designated on these account. They are sold through banks and trust companies as well as insurance companies.	Non Registered account CAN have a beneficiary listed. You can list both primary and secondary beneficiaries on these accounts. Great for estate planning. Provided only through insurance companies.
Without a spouse, the only option is to leave these assets to the estate for distribution or to hold them jointly with someone else. This could create a situation where assets get exposed to creditors or simply exposed to the joint owner.	No matter the situation, these assets remain under the control of the owner. Upon death, they flow through the named beneficiaries, no matter how many there might be. No cause for legal fees, extra time or probate taxes. Assets become liquid quickly upon death.

So the first thing you will do is open an AA for yourself. If you recently lost a loved one, you can deposit your insurance cheque in there and forget about it, and go back to doing what is most important, looking after yourself and the process of properly mourning your loss.

It will earn some interest, and if you want to withdraw or draw against it that can also be arranged.

Unlike GICs, with an AA you can designate beneficiaries, which can be individuals, charities or any other entity you wish. Because you have named the beneficiary of your money, it does not go to your estate when you leave us, thus saving probate, legal fees and time.

There are many more reasons to consider AAs over and above those already mentioned. Let me explain a couple of the most important.

Banks often try to "help clients out" by offering to hold bank accounts and investments jointly with children if there are no spouses available. I appreciate the effort, but unless the child has no spouse, no debt, no friends, and no siblings, and not in business for themselves, that might not be a good idea.

Joint account holders bring their "baggage" to the situation. If I have a joint account with my son and he gets married, I just gave half my assets to him and his wife as part of their assets. I also gave their creditors access to half of my assets as well. I realize we all know our families inside and out (tongue firmly pressed against cheek) but financial planning is not the testing ground for your background knowledge.

Enter the AA. You own it all. All the time. When you leave us, there is one beneficiary or many. These can be changed. Often or never. No one has control of your money while invested other than you.

If you wish, you can even put in a contingent plan — backup plan, panic room, whatever you want to call it. You can plan for it. And all the while you keep control of the asset.

When you are no longer with us, the money goes directly to those named by you in the contract. Outside of the estate. No legal fees. No delays. Maybe some taxes depending on what the asset is, but quicker and easier than ***any*** other bank product. Period.

Now, as your GICs come up for renewal, you move them to the AAs, removing them from involvement with your estate. Because there is no limit to the amount you have in an AA, you can actually put everything you have in there, which means in the event of your death it will go straight to the beneficiary you named, with no delay and no question.

If you are not interested in guaranteed interest rates, there is another solution the insurance companies have, called Segregated Funds. These are the Mutual Fund equivalent that offer the same beneficiary benefits of the AA but in a market based investment. Definitely worth exploring if you are in any of the situations outlined above for the AA estate plan.

Over the course of my career in financial services I have shared this concept with many people who hold assets in traditional GIC investments. One would think that based on this knowledge and the number of times I have shared it that I would have an incredible amount of money invested in AAs for clients. Not the case. Crazy right? Here are a few reasons I think people continue to use what they have become accustomed to.

Reason one is people have become accustomed and comfortable. Comfort food, comfort investments I guess. To go with what you know is way easier than trying to figure something new. Another reason might be that these types of investments can't just be moved over all at once. They are invested for multiple layers over multiple years in most cases. So it will take as long as the longest term that the money is currently invested in.

That last reason assumes the product, concept, company and advisor makes it through this next stumbling point. Family and friends. Yes, you read that correctly, I said family and friends could be the reason why someone decides not to use an AA for their investments.

You see, the target market, if I could use the term to help bring this home, is someone who is often seen as someone who needs assistance in planning their finances whether that is true or not. For example, Dad passes away and Mom is now receiving input from all her children, siblings, friends and neighbours. All, of course, want the best and believe they are helping the situation. Best intentions of course. In reality, what is happening is an increasing level of confusion that ultimately leads to doing nothing at all of what Mom is accustomed to and comfortable with. So you can see the circle of life here and why most stay with what they know.

The majority of people I deal with in this regard are parents or relatives of those I have already been able to help put this concept in place. They are able to share the idea at a high level using examples they are personally familiar with. That also makes the introduction to an advisor that understands the concepts and products they are describing that much easier.

Although it is best to engage in a relationship with an advisor when there are no outside stresses or influences, it doesn't mean that if you don't have one during these times that it is too late to get one. A financial planner can have the greatest impact during these stressful times so it is worth the effort to find one even then.

13

TWO BIG MYTHS AND TWO GREAT TRUTHS

Big Myth No. 1

When you choose an executor to handle your estate, you don't have to tell them. It will be a nice surprise.

The Truth

The job of being an executor is not what it's cracked up to be. Unfortunately, for the person to be at the point of taking over their duties as executor or trustee, they will have just lost someone they care about. In a lot of cases they end up stumbling through it and trying their best to honour a loved one. That is why I always ask people to put themselves in the "***shoes of the problem***" in order to decide if they are making the right choices or not.

What I mean by that is, put yourself in the position of

executor of someone's estate and see how you feel. Your parent or spouse has just passed away. You are emotionally crushed by that event and at that same moment, you are given the job of settling the financial affairs of your loved one.

If that isn't enough to make it a terrible job, consider this. Executors take on Unlimited Lifetime Liability. I'll say that again: ***Unlimited. Lifetime. Liability.*** Just three words, but pretty heavy duty when you put them together.

It's not such a big deal if you are the executor and the sole beneficiary — unless you plan on suing yourself that is. But it can be a very large issue if there are others besides yourself involved in the estate.

Often when people lose a loved one, in my experience, they can also lose a strain of DNA! OK so they don't actually lose it, but there seems to be one in most families, crowds, beneficiary lists etc. who immediately takes issue with everything and everyone. Goes crazy! That is why I refer to it as losing a strain of DNA. (If you don't think your family has someone crazy like that in it, it might just be you!) Executors have to be prepared to work with those people, or at least protect themselves from them.

When people find out they are beneficiaries in an estate, they become very interested in what is happening in the process of settling that estate. In some cases, they might ***not*** even ***be*** a beneficiary but believe they ***could*** be, and their interest level goes up anyway!

This is why it is so important to choose your executor wisely — and also to understand your role as executor if you have been appointed as one.

You can't keep this kind of appointment a secret. I strongly recommend you tell those you appoint in your will and power of attorney even before you sign off on those documents. Let them know you are considering them for the roles and see how they react. Watch and listen to them as you continue to talk about your plans for them. You will get a good idea at that point if you are making the best decision on not. Better to know now than later.

Of course if we are talking about your executor, you will be deceased, so who cares? I would imagine there are some who might care, or you probably wouldn't be preparing your will or discussing these issues at all.

I refer to this group as your ***Estate Team***, and just as with any other team, you must pick your players wisely. Just because you put them into your will and name them as executor, that doesn't mean they ***will*** act as executor. There is a window of time between a death and carrying out the first duty of an executor during which they can back out of the job. If you didn't have a back-up plan in your will, your estate could be held up for a very long time as lawyers and those beneficiaries duke it out over who gets what and why. In fact, everyone will get less in that situation — except, of course, the lawyers.

Share your wishes. Tell everyone you appoint to your ***Estate Team*** that they got the part. You might find out pretty quickly that they didn't really want the role to begin with. If that is the case, it would take away any of the benefits you gain from having a proper will in place. Quite honestly, if you are worried about telling them when you are alive and well, things might not be any better after you are gone. If that is the case, you might want to rethink who you chose for those roles. This process should not be likened to choosing your bridal party, but unfortunately people often treat it that way.

It is important to go through the process of creating a will or power of attorney at many different times throughout your life. Each time you do, choosing your ***Estate Team*** should be a high priority. Having the proper skills and personalities in place to complete these tasks is of utmost importance.

The majority of wills are not created until people are married, and in fact after they have children. I'm not suggesting that is the right way to approach your estate planning, but it can often be a simpler process. With a spouse to roll everything over to, the beneficiary and the executor may be one and the same, and the roster of your ***Estate Team*** is also often smaller. That statement was not intended to give permission to wait, but to let those who haven't already done this planning know that it is never too late.

It is important to note that if you created a will while living with someone common-law and then married that person, your will became null and void at the time of the marriage, unless the marriage was mentioned in the will when it was written. So this is one of those times when you would want to revisit your wishes and your estate.

A truth not universally known is that if you have a properly executed will and then you get married, the will becomes void.

Consider the second marriage of a business owner who doesn't realize this and dies intestate. Imagine the surprise of those left behind when they find out that the best laid plans that were put in place are now null and void.

The consequences of dying intestate for a business owner as opposed to anyone else are only magnified by size and complexity.

Just a few of the many other times when it is prudent to revisit your estate wishes are: death of a spouse, purchase or sale of a property, sale of a business, sale of any assets that may have been listed in the will, the addition or subtraction of family members. Or you may want to change your will simply because of changes in relationships with those you have listed in your will.

Even if none of the above situations happen to you, that doesn't mean you should never review your will. In fact, it is wise practice to get out your will every few years to look it over. You may have forgotten something that you had added to the will, or you may noticed there is a change in the age of the beneficiary that makes an existing trustee no longer necessary.

There could also be changes to the *Family Law Act* which could make some wills work very differently than was envisioned when they were first drafted. A trusted financial advisor will be able to help you review things and identify items you might need to discuss further with your lawyer.

Creating a good will and set of power of attorney documents is only step one. After that, make sure those who are listed in those documents are aware of their duties, as well as the location of important documents and trusted advisors they can work with. Having everything well documented and easy to understand will help your ***Estate Team*** do their job more easily.

Shortly after I lost my Dad, our family kept saying things like, "Would Dad have liked this?" Or "Where is the.....?" That's what drove me soon after to create a document called ***The Family Registry***. Many companies over the years have created their own paper versions of similar documents and given them away to people to help them in the planning process. What I was seeing is that most people either filled it out immediately and never updated it again, which takes away the value of the document, or they simply didn't use it at all.

I took steps to make the document easier for people to use.

My version of *The Family Registry* is a pdf that you can fill out on your computer or tablet, and you can print copies to give to your Estate Team. You can also save it to update later, which makes the process of keeping it up to date that much easier.

It is ***not*** meant to act as a will, but rather a basis for the discussion and gathering of information so that you can properly create a will. It also allows you to gather the information in one place to help those listed on your Estate Team. You can download the Family Registry on my website, billmcbay.com. There are also other helpful items there that I update regularly as I find more useful information that I believe is worth sharing.

Is Fair Equal or is Equal Fair?

This question is asked a lot in the process of estate planning. For example, a son has worked on the farm ever since he can remember. A daughter moves away and lives out of town and has her own career and family. Should the entire estate, including the farm, be split down the middle? Or does the son get the farm and slightly less of the other assets, and the daughter overall less, because the farm is such a large part of the value of the estate? There is no right or wrong answer to this question. It is a personal discussion and an important one.

I would suggest that in this case, 50/50 between the two is equal, but might not be fair. But would the daughter agree? You know what they say about the best laid plans? Let me tell you, they might not be so good if the plans come as a surprise when mom and dad are no longer around. I have seen fully functioning families fall out over situations very similar to what I am explaining here.

Of course, those who plan their estate properly are usually doing so to ensure everyone is looked after and that there are no hard feelings. If this question is not answered properly and then shared with those whom it involves prior to your death, it could create a very difficult and messy situation.

Let me go back to the beginning of this section and remind you about the ***Unlimited Lifetime Liability***. If the child who is considered to be favoured by the will is also the executor, the other child could tie the estate up in legal battles for a long time. This would create more stress and legal costs that no one wants or needs. All because of the strain of DNA that is now missing along with the definition of Equal and Fair not being properly understood by all members of the family or the Estate Team.

Unfortunately, this or similar scenarios happen all the time. So much so that insurance companies have recently found a way to insure executors against the risk of being sued. Executor Insurance is purchased by the executor within the first 60 days of death. The cost for the insurance is most often paid through the estate as part of the fees that an executor can charge for their services. If the estate is not large enough to cover the cost but the liability of being sued is thought to be large, the executor can always pay for the coverage personally.

Some people are actually adding a clause to their will saying that Executor Insurance is to be purchased with the premiums being paid by the estate funds. I believe this will become more and more the norm as this type of insurance becomes better known and understood.

When I talk to people about this I get some very different reactions, the most common one being that it is sad we are at a place where executors are being sued. Of course I completely agree with that statement, but we live in a litigious society and, in the vernacular of today, “it is what it is.” So we protect ourselves and our loved ones from whatever we can. This insurance and proper planning is just one way to do so.

So the second Truth is that suddenly finding out you are a loved one’s executor after he or she dies is not a nice surprise, and in fact can be a nasty shock. Tell the person you have appointed them executor. In fact, it might be a good idea to ask them first if they are willing to serve.

Grandpa at the Retirement Home

New relationships don't always have to be early in your life; they can also happen later on in life.

Let's look at Grandpa George for example. George had lost his wife, Charlotte, a few years earlier and decided it was time to sell the house that he and Charlotte had lived in for their entire life together. His children were all grown up and had successful lives of their own. He sold his home and decided to consider a retirement residence.

After he sold the house but before it closed, he realized

that was one of those life changing events his financial planner always spoke of and he sat down with his planner to go over the new plan with the proceeds of the house. He needed to better understand how he was going to pay for his new living expenses. The plan was done and his planner suggested that he also take this time to get his will updated to reflect the new plan.

He wanted to ensure that his children would get the proceeds of his estate quickly and easily and with as little tax as possible. Seems like a good enough idea and easily done with some proper planning and a new will.

George thrived in this new community. He got the bounce back in his step. The kids enjoyed seeing their Dad come back to life. He hadn't really been the same since Mom passed away and this was the first glimpse of their Dad coming around.

Other people noticed Dad as well. Not only did he get a number of new friends that he could play pool and cards with, he also turned the head of a certain lady friend as well.

Margaret had lost her husband around the same time as George lost Charlotte. They had a lot in common and enjoyed spending countless hours together. Both Margaret and George had grown children who could all see how happy they made each other. It just seemed like the next step to get married and enter the second phase of their life together.

Both Margaret and George believed in proper estate planning and both set up their estates to go to their children and grandchildren as they didn't require anything from one another. This marriage was entirely about their new found love and not any financial need.

Being both caught up in the excitement of the wedding, and understanding that they both had new wills done before moving into their new retirement communities, they didn't see any need to reach out to their lawyers or financial planners.

Shortly after the wedding, George started to show signs of dementia. Margaret was very supporting and cared for George as long as she could, but unfortunately Margaret died suddenly of a massive heart attack.

It wasn't until then that the family understood the situation that they were in. Margaret was deemed to have passed away intestate, without a valid will. The will she created to ensure her assets would go to her kids was considered void upon her marriage to George.

As she had died intestate, the value of her estate would eventually flow to her spouse, George. This is where the problem was realized. George's will was also void due to their marriage and now he does not have the mental capacity to make a new one. So all his and Margaret's assets will flow down to ***his*** children after a lengthy process of settling the estate of a descendant who was intestate.

George's children could be very nice and make sure that everything is given to Margaret's children, but they certainly don't have to. What if they secretly didn't like Margaret but only supported the marriage because it made their Dad happy? The list of what could happen in this situation is long. Not to mention the legal fees that surround each one.

This situation happens more often than one would expect. I share this story with you in order for you to start thinking about your own situation. Do you have things in place? Are they still in place? Will they be in place no matter your mental capacity or marital status?

Planning once and then forgetting about it will not work. Plans need to be updated and tweaked as life goes on, right up until the end.

Big Myth No. 2

I don't need a will — I don't have anything.

The Truth

Now there is a Big Myth if I ever heard one. The truth is that everyone over 18 years old should have a will. The type of will can be determined based on the level of "stuff" or family dynamics, but a will is for everyone.

Let me give you just a couple of scenarios that demonstrate why this is true.

Family Disaster

A family, including Mom, Dad, 18-year-old child and last living grandparent, are all killed in a common disaster. Assuming that Grandma and the parents have up-to-date wills that account for common disasters, the residual of Grandma's estate is left to her son, aka Dad, and any of his siblings depending on her will. Dad's portion will go to Mom, assuming he is older. That now leaves everything to the 18-year-old child. Of course the child doesn't have a will — he's just a kid after all, he "doesn't have anything."

Because of that one fact — the 18-year-old dying intestate — the estate of both parents and the part of Grandma's estate that Dad received will all now be locked up in a legal process of determining who gets what and how much. Throw in the fact that it is an accident and that some insurers will require more information and time to settle the claim, and the lack of access to cash to keep the payments running on the house and other large assets that require financial attention, and you have a very expensive and long process in the hands of some unknown person who has yet to be determined.

If the son *had* had a will, he would more than likely have gone through the exercise of choosing someone to be his executor. Any lawyer would have suggested Mom and Dad first, but would also have suggested choosing someone else to act as secondary in the event of exactly what we are discussing. Even if it was an uncle or aunt or cousin, at least the thought process of who it should be would have been gone through and things would be working a lot more smoothly and less expensively in this case.

I understand that my example is a little extreme. You can't plan for everything. I mean really, what about a war or a virus or something similar? It has to stop somewhere. If that's what you are thinking, here's a completely different situation that might change your mind.

Everybody Has "Stuff"

Think kids have no "stuff"? Think again. Many young people have digital assets and intellectual property that have a value no-one ever considers.

Let's say, for example, your son started a Twitter account with such a cool concept he was soon able to gain tens of thousands, if not hundreds of thousands, of followers. You, or even your son, may think that's not such a big deal, but it does in fact have value. Such value needs to be listed, and account passwords need to be available to the Estate Team in the event of the account holder's death.

Not only is a will necessary, but this is another reason to complete a Family Registry. It's one thing to stumble across a coin collection in a closet while cleaning out your late uncle's house — you'd probably know how to go about figuring out its value. But what if you stumbled across a printed email with confirmation of purchase of an internet domain from GoDaddy™. Would you know how to find out how much that is worth?

These domain names, or URLs, can in fact be extremely valuable, and collecting them — sometimes known as URL squatting — has become quite popular. For example there is a well documented story of some young kids who purchased 21centuryfox.com and every other version of the name, and then sold it to the then 20th Century Fox for an undisclosed sum of money. Each URL probably cost them less than $20 but carried a much higher value to a company that was considering what to do when the calendar switched over to the 21st Century. Those kids certainly had some "stuff"!

So does your son or daughter own anything of value digitally? Or will it become of value? It could even be pictures they have taken and posted on a Facebook page, or an actual Facebook page or other social media property. There's gold in them thar hills — or at least there could be. So going through the process of creating a will or completing the Family Registry is worthwhile for anyone at any age. You might be surprised to find that while you thought your kids were just wasting time online, they were actually creating something of value.

Executor Beware!

Again, I should point out the liability to the executor if they don't properly understand this part of their duties. If my executor, for example is not aware of my URL collection, or understand the value of royalties, trademarks and copyrights, they might not properly value them. This could result in an undervaluation of my estate and create the potential exposure to litigation by one or many of my beneficiaries at some future date.

Assets are not always listed on statements or made of bricks and mortar. They come in all different shapes and sizes, and as the owner you should understand yours and detail them in your will or at least share some information about them with your executor.

If, on the other hand, you are acting as someone's executor, you must properly value them for the beneficiaries you are representing — whether or not you are one of them. That is why listing passwords to online sites is just as important as knowing where the will or the keys to safety deposit box are located.

Please be careful how you list these passwords though. If not done properly while you are still living, it certainly could make living your life difficult. Unfortunately, during both life and death we must be aware of possibilities that might expose us to identity theft.

The plot thickens, for everyone!

Let's say there are online accounts that someone has when they pass away. Let's also say that someone we will call Mr. Fraudster figures out a way to hack into those accounts and pretend to be that person before the executor can notify everyone. Let's even say that the executor doesn't even realize online websites and accounts are of any value, so they don't even start the process of closing them down. The entire value of the deceased's estate could be lost due to identity theft right under the executor's eyes without anyone knowing until it is too late.

Our society is becoming incredibly digital in so many

ways. Consider not only social networking that often tells the world our every thought, consideration, challenge or failure. But there is so much more. Something as small as forwarding jokes and not using blind carbon copy (bcc) so it shares with the world all your friends' email addresses. Not a big deal right? Wrong! That is the first step in gathering a profile of the person Mr. Fraudster might want to become. It was once explained to me that email is like sending postcards. Very easy to look at during the mail process and the message is never secure. That explanation stuck with me, I hope it does to you as well. That is why it is so important to be careful throughout life and for executors after we're gone.

The forwarding of jokes is such a small thing, so why all the fuss?

From reading the emails that people send, you can get an idea of words or phrases that are used often, the friends they are sent to and what those people also enjoy and find funny. It might also give those who read it an idea of the age of the person and what that person likes or dislikes.

That is before they even searched out your social network pages. You know, the ones that you left open to the world because you didn't use the proper security. From those pages they can find out even more about how you live your life. What political party you follow, maybe religion or family structure.

By looking at your unsecured photos they might even see where you live, work and travel to. Every picture has something called a geotag associated with it. If you haven't set your camera to ***not*** share that or your website settings to keep that private, someone can quite quickly figure out where you live and when you will be there or not there, based on the patterns they witness from your posts they see on-line.

I'm not trying to scare you. Okay, maybe just a bit. That is what it takes sometimes to make a change. Health scare: eat and live better. Driving accident you survive: phone goes in purse where it can't be reached. The list goes on and on. But consider this story of Uncle Jim to see how it might apply.

We sure miss Uncle Jim

It came as a major shock when we lost Uncle Jim. He had been the life of the party and favourite uncle, friend and colleague to many. Jim had done well in business over the course of his lifetime. His personality was magnetic. Personally and professionally he was loved by many. So it was not a big surprise that he had a large circle of friends.

Uncle Jim was also very tech savvy for his age, not an old man by any stretch of the imagination. At age 63 after being retired for just over three years, he was online and networking socially at an above-average pace. He had shared many photos and videos of family and friends he shared some amazing trips with.

He also hosted many parties at his lovely home, which were also shared all over his social network. His social network became very large as he didn't secure who could see things on his page. His philosophy was always that he would rather share with many than to forget someone. A way of life that made him exactly the great man he was.

So you could imagine that when we heard of his passing, everyone was in total shock. There was an outpouring of sympathy on line. Sharing of pictures and videos that were shared current and from many years ago. You could be said that sympathy for Jim went viral on his social networks in the days following his death.

No one ever thought of anything other than sadness for his loss, and happiness as they shared memories of his life on line. So you can imagine the feelings of anger combined with sadness that was felt when the family came home after the funeral to a house that had been ransacked. Every item of value, monetary and personal, was gone or broken.

It was as if the criminals knew exactly when to come, how long they would have and what to take. That's because they did. They had been watching sympathy pour out on line for Uncle Jim. They realized they should take a closer look.

They saw travel videos that showed Uncle Jim and Aunt Sue enjoying times with friends and family. They noticed jewelry that they both wore. Pictures from the retirement party held at the house further intrigued the crooks as they showed beautiful art and significant investments in technology. They didn't need to see a safe or coin collections at that point, they had enough intelligence.

Then the obituary was published with information about where it was, what type of a man he was, how successful he was in his career. It also outlined the visitation and funeral times and with a quick internet search of the distance and time between the funeral home and the residence, they knew the window they had. A quick reference back to social media to confirm whether or not they own a dog and bingo, the drive-by was planned.

Probably started similar to the Christmas movie, *Home Alone*. A door bell is rung and no one shows up. Game on.

There are not many silver linings to this story, if any, but let me see if I can find one when it comes to executor duties and liability.

In this story, Aunt Sue was still living and the sole beneficiary and executor of Uncle Jim's estate. As terrible a situation as this is, it was not magnified by the fact that if the executor had to deal with other beneficiaries, they would have opened themselves up to litigation. Under the watch of the executor, the value of the estate was decreased.

I'm not saying every situation will end in the courts. I hope they don't. But if this did, it would be difficult to explain how this was not the executor's fault.

So how do you protect yourself from a situation like this without burning your computer? Here are some hints.

Never leave an empty home during the visitation or funeral. Have people take shifts if need be. Update and review your privacy settings on all your social media websites regularly. Those two items will help a lot for sure. Someone once told me you can't prevent the winds from blowing or the waves from crashing. Very true statement. So just do what you can to be careful on a windy day, and don't turn your back to waves in the ocean.

Angie and Phil – a story about how timing really is everything.

When I met with Angie and Phil at their home, Angie was not feeling well. She had been suffering from flu-like symptoms from earlier that afternoon, but because we had booked the appointment some time in advance and they knew it was important, they didn't want to cancel.

We discussed everything from their plans to start a family, buy a house, start a business, and finally their retirement. We were all over the map. Blue sky thinking on a number of different topics.

At the end of our meeting the one thing we knew for sure was that they needed to put in place some life insurance so that if one of them didn't reach the goal, the other still could. So we applied for an amount that would cover the mortgage they didn't have yet, the school for the children they didn't have yet and pay for the cost of one of them no longer being here.

Turned out, the timing was immaculate. When Angie's flu-like symptoms got worse and the headaches unbearable, they went to the hospital. She was quickly put through a number of tests, which produced the ultimate "good news/bad news" results.

The good news: they were pregnant and expecting their first child. The bad news: Angie had a brain tumor that needed to be operated on immediately.

She had crossed the insurance line. She was officially uninsurable. What started out as flu-type symptoms only too quickly turned into vastly different outcomes. Pregnant and battling a cancerous brain tumor, and all within 100 hours since applying for life insurance.

What happened to that application? Well it was approved without any issue of course. At the time of application, to the best of their knowledge she answered the questions truthfully and honestly. The company was able to ask for additional information if they required, and all was good.

They just got in under the wire — even though they didn't even know there was a wire to get in under.

14

THE FINAL MYTH

As I write this second edition, we are in the midst of our fight against Covid-19, and we continue to see stock markets fluctuate greatly due to the current state of uncertainty. I think it's important to concentrate on what "certainties" we have available to us.

The old saying, "You can't stop the waves from crashing" can be related to our current situation. Beaches are some of the most beautiful places in the world, I think we would all agree. On most days that is. But those days when the wind gets strong and the tides are high they can also be very dangerous.

On those bad days it's not usually a good idea to wade into the water and toss the football around. Heck, it's not even a good idea to lie on the beach or go anywhere near the water. Best to just stay clear and let it pass, because we can't stop it. We know from storms gone by that it will pass. The sun will come back out and the waves will be of normal size — and back in we go, football and all!

These trying times are very similar to that. We need to let

the market do what it does. What it has always done. Nothing we do will stop it.

The advice I am giving to my clients today is no different to my advice of the past, because the message remains the same. Stay in, and always keep your hands and feet in the cart until it comes to a complete stop.

But is there anything else you can do to make the ride a bit better? For sure there is, and I want to share a few things you can do, or at least consider, to make this crazy time a bit less crazy.

1) If you are at the stage of withdrawing from your investments, reduce your income draw if at all possible.

In this current environment it's safe to say we are all spending a bit less. No travel. No eating out. No entertaining, etc. So, if those savings can be applied against what you're drawing from your investments, that will ultimately help.

2) Continue or increase your regular contributions.

If you are contributing regularly to your investments, now is not the time to stop that. In fact, if anything, increase what you are depositing into your investments. Use the same concept to the income statement above, by applying the savings from your current lifestyle to your investments. This will ensure you are buying more investment units while the market is lower, thus helping your overall balance sheet when the markets correct.

3) Stop logging on to your accounts on line to check balances.

Probably the most important things you can do are not open your statements when they arrive and stop looking on line to see how things are going. The only thing I can promise you is that this will drive you crazy.

People often ask me who my biggest competitor is. I tell

them it's my client's gut, neighbours, family members or the person they work closest to. It's not surprising that in times of uncertainty, people listen to those they trust. I just suggest that whether it's a trusted friend or trusted co-worker, their message might be different than your trusted financial advisor.

4) Trigger unrealized capital losses in any non-registered or OPEN accounts if they exist.

One silver lining in a volatile market is the ability to trigger an otherwise unrealized capital loss. That's basically the difference between the Adjusted Cost Base (ACB or Book Value) of your investments and their current market value. In markets like the one we are experiencing currently, there are sometimes situations where the market value is lower than the ACB. If that is the case, it is referred to as an unrealized loss.

To realize the loss, you need to sell the funds you hold at that time to another investment for a period of no less than 30 days. (There is additional strategy here that is unique to each investor.) This will trigger a capital loss in the eyes of CRA, and you will receive a tax slip that will allow you to deduct the loss from any gains in that calendar year. If you have no gains in the current calendar year, you can carry these losses forward indefinitely, and also apply to any gains back three years. So the real benefit here is that future gains will be offset.

5) If possible, use your Tax-Free Savings Account (TFSA) if you're planning to "buy in" during this market low.

If you can invest funds at this time at these record market lows, then I suggest you do it inside your TFSA if you have room. Here's why. The reason you are taking advantage of market lows is to make back what they have lost, in this case up to 20% in some cases. So, if you make that much return, you certainly don't want to pay taxes on it as that will ultimately reduce the amount you get to keep. The TFSA is 100%

tax free, so it's very safe for you to use to reduce taxes you may need to pay on that growth.

Then the second step to this approach is to remove these funds from the TFSA once they have increased in value and deposit them into your RSP. That will not only save you taxes on the growth but get you a tax return from your regular income for the contribution to your RSP.

Not only will you get a tax deduction based on your marginal tax rate, you will also get all the TFSA room back the next time the calendar flips to January 1st again.

So there are a few certainties that may apply to you during this volatile time. If you have any questions about them or want to see how they might affect your personal situation, call your advisor to discuss them.

Although I have been discussing Covid-19, as that is fresh in everyone's at the time of publishing this book, the concepts here can be applied at any time for any market fluctuations that may occur in the future.

15

IN CLOSING

I hope this book has helped you understand at least this Big Truth: in order to take at least some control of your destiny, you ***do*** need a financial plan and you ***do*** need to do it right away. It should be at the top of your priority list for your life. Don't wait too long to start the conversation, because that is really all it is — a conversation.

The fact that you started by just reading this book is part of the planning process. I urge you to become educated in what affects your life. Of course, financial planning is just one aspect of your life, but it certainly affects many other parts if done rightly or wrongly.

If you don't yet work with a financial planner, please reference the list of interview questions on pages 19-21 and start your search immediately. Put your Estate Team together and share your goals with them. Make sure your loved ones are looked after and have the newfound knowledge you have acquired through this book.

When I started this project over six years ago, my goal was to create a way to get what I believe to be very important information into the hands of those who require it, *when* they require it. What came from that goal was this book, a book I hope will be given to family and friends as a gift at different life changing events throughout their lives. Maybe even handed down from parents to children as they grow wings and start off on their own. A tool to help someone you care about without having to say a word.

My hope is that you are thankful for the time you invested in reading this book and that you might take even just one thing from it to better your situation financially. If that is the case, I have accomplished my goal.

Good luck with your planning and may you, as a certain well known space explorer once said, "Live Long and Prosper!"

Bill

APPENDIX I

LIST OF DESIGNATIONS OF FINANCIAL PLANNERS IN CANADA

CFP - Certified Financial Planner

This is the premier designation for financial planners. The CFP designation is recognized internationally for excellence in financial planning. There are approximately 17,000 CFP professionals across Canada, part of an international network of 175,000 individuals who have earned CFP certification in 26 territories around the world. Any advisor with this designation can act as your financial coach to put the rest of the team together for you. They will have a great depth of knowledge in all aspects of financial planning and will know who to bring in to help, and when. The CFP is administered by FP Canada, which operates as a non-profit organization. Their sole mission is to increase the level of knowledge of financial planners in the countries they serve. www.fpcanada.ca

QAFP - Qualified Associate Financial Planner

Qualified Associate Financial Planner™ certification replaced FPSC Level 1® certification, and all current FPSC Level 1 certificants became QAFP professionals.

QAFP™ certification demonstrates a financial planner's competence and commitment to the highest ethical standards of responsibility. QAFP professionals have demonstrated the knowledge, skills, experience and ethics to provide holistic financial planning strategies and solutions for average Canadians with typical financial planning needs. www.fpcanada.ca

CLU - Chartered Life Underwriter

Original designation dating back to 1924. The CLU advisor's knowledge and application skills are in three key areas of wealth transfer and estate planning advice. They will determine the effect of income tax regulations on the client's financial needs and objectives, recognize the impact of the laws of the various jurisdictions that affect the rights and obligations of their clients in financial and estate planning and identify problems, gather comprehensive data, and plan integrated solutions. www.iafe.ca

CHS - Certified Health Specialist

These advisors have expertise in all areas of health insurance, including income replacement, critical illness, long-term care, disability and group benefits. This designation will eventually replace the RHU — Registered Health Underwriter — in Canada. www.iafe.ca

CEA - Certified Executor Advisor

A Certified Executor Advisor (CEA) is an accredited specialist advising Canadian executors using a team-oriented networking approach. They have specialized skills in all areas of wrapping up an estate in order to help executors.

Their relationships with experts in these areas help them provide executors with general guidance while providing comprehensive support as and when needed. www.cicea.ca

FDS - Chartered Financial Divorce Specialist

The FDS is an accredited financial planner who has received specialized training in matters relating to separation and divorce in order to provide an objective assessment for potential scenarios. www.afds.ca

TEP - Trust and Estate Practitioner

The Trust and Estate Practitioner designation (TEP) is a worldwide recognized designation and is a way to formally identify qualified practitioners and distinguish them from non-specialists who occasionally deal with trusts and estates. Unlike the CEA, these advisors work to ensure things are set up properly prior to death. www.step.ca

CPA - Chartered Professional Accountant

In October 2014 CPA became the single premier designation for Accounting Professionals in Canada. The **CA - Chartered Accountant** and the **CGA - Certified General Accountant** were combined together as CPA. www.cpacanada.ca

CFA - Chartered Financial Analyst

The Chartered Financial Analyst (CFA) is a professional credential offered internationally by the American-based CFA Institute to investment and financial professionals. It covers a broad range of topics relating to investment management, financial analysis, stocks, bonds and derivatives, and provides a generalist knowledge of other areas of finance. www.c-fainstitue.org

CHFC - Chartered Financial Consultant

This designation is very similar to the CFP when it comes to specialties covered and general knowledge. The CHFC has a few more courses to take but does not have the final exam that the CFP has. They are somewhat competing designations, so it is fair to say they will always evolve to be viewed similarly by the public with regards to content and specialties. www.iafe.ca

RRC - Registered Retirement Consultant

Advisors with the comprehensive knowledge to focus on retirement concepts and strategies. www.retirementinstitute.ca

CIM - Chartered Investment Manager

This designation was previously the Canadian Investment Manager. These advisors are educated to create and manage portfolios of investments for their clients. They are approved to carry out discretionary portfolio management by the Canadian Securities Administrator. www.csi.ca

CRC - Certified Retirement Counselor

This is a relatively new designation that is similar in focus to the RRC outlined above. www.cifp.ca

CPCA - The Certified Professional Consultant on Aging

This designation is known as the **CSA - Certified Senior Advisor** in the U.S. The designation course provides an overview of the health, social, financial, and legal considerations that arise as we navigate our various life stages. These advisors have the skills to work with you through not only the financial side of aging, but also understand some of the other challenges to help as well. www.cpcacanada.com

EPC - Elder Planning Counselor

Designed to provide the essential knowledge and tools necessary to effectively develop proper rapport and practical solutions. Anyone who works in the 50+ market can hold this designation, not just Financial Planners. www.cieps.com

DFA - Tax Services Specialist

The practical application of tax legislation and interpretation. Skills include the preparation of taxes, bookkeeping, cross-border taxation and tax strategies. www.knowledgebureau.com

PFP - Personal Financial Planner

This designation was created originally for the banks and recently was taken over by CSI Global Education Inc. They are attempting to make it better to somewhat compete with the CFP designation which is the largest in Canada and run by FP Canada, a non-profit organization. You will find these designated Advisors mostly in banks or with a bank background. www.csi.ca

CIWM - Certified International Wealth Manager

Diverse disciplines required to serve the integrated wealth management needs of high-net-worth clients, including trust strategy and succession planning, insurance, tax strategy and estate planning. www.csi.ca

MTI - Estate and Trust Professional

How to protect, invest and distribute estate and trust assets. All administrative procedures for settling estates and managing ongoing trusts as well as effective risk mitigation for trustees and executors. www.csi.ca

As you can see, there are many to choose from. I'm positive there are even more that end up on the business cards of advisors that I haven't even listed or heard of. The landscape of the financial planning industry is changing and evolving all the time. So you will see more consolidation in these designations over time. You will also more than likely see a large push for more promotion of the designations that should be on every advisor's business card. These are all very positive changes to ensure our clients are protected and well informed to make better choices.

APPENDIX II

DEFINITIONS YOU SHOULD UNDERSTAND

The financial industry is also riddled with acronyms that help to confuse those the products they refer to were intended to help in the first place. Here are a few that you might stumble across in your path to financial freedom.

CII – Critical Illness Insurance

Coverage that pays a cash benefit upon the survival of a listed critical illness, for example heart attack, cancer or stroke. The amount it pays is tax free and can be used for anything the beneficiary wants. Originally intended to ensure survivors didn't have to dip into their registered retirement savings to pay for alternative health care or to live out last days without the worry of financial stress, but has paid for many Disney trips since then.

LTCI – Long Term Care Insurance

Coverage that pays a weekly amount of money after the insured is unable to perform any two of the six activities of daily living (bathing, feeding, dressing, transferring, continence and toileting). Income type products allow the funds to be used for anything the insured wishes, including paying family members to help perform those duties. Reimbursement type products, do just that, reimburse you for expenses incurred for care during that time in your life.

CPP – Canada Pension Plan

Government pension based on the amount of contributions a Canadian makes over his or her working career. 50% of the contributions are made by the employer, the other 50% by the employee. Self-employed Canadians pay both sides of the contributions. https://www.canada.ca/en/services/benefits/publicpensions/cpp.html

OAS – Old age Security

Government pension based on the number of years you lived in Canada. No contributions required. 40 years is a full pension. Amount is reduced based on a clawback system. The more you make, the more they take back. It is important to plan so that you can receive this if possible. If you consider this a tax refund then you will make TFSA, Non-Registered and tax preferred investments your friend. Remember, it all comes from the same bank account, so why not consider all Government benefits as a tax refund. https://www.canada.ca/en/services/benefits/publicpensions/cpp/old-age-security.html

RRSP – Registered Retirement Savings Plan

Type of investment vehicle that creates a tax deduction in the current tax year. When money is taken as income or lump sum withdrawal, it is all 100% taxable as income. Great tax planning tool if used properly. Key word is properly. Understanding your marginal tax rate during your working career and how it compares to that of your retirement will ensure you are using it properly.

http://www.cra-arc.gc.ca/tx/ndvdls/tpcs/rrsp-reer/rrsps-eng.html

RESP – Registered Education Plan

Type of investment vehicle which, when money is deposited into the account, can qualify for a 20% Canadian Education Savings Grant (CESG) along with other money from the Government based on earned income of the account owner. Lower income Canadians could qualify for other grants and bonds that will increase the value of this product for them.

http://www.cra-arc.gc.ca/tx/ndvdls/tpcs/resp-reee/menu-eng.html

LIRA – Locked-In Retired Account

A version of the RRSP that is locked in, and where proceeds from former pensions funds end up. Locked in with little to no access until age 55 unless you fall under financial hardship. Provincial legislation governs how each account works. In some cases they can also be federally regulated depending on the scope of the employer where the funds originated. Refer to the government website that regulates your account for more information.

LIF – Life Income Fund

This is where a LIRA grows up to become an income. Currently, locked in funds must be transferred into a LIF no later than December of the year you turn 71 years old. The income stream has minimums and maximums, unlike the RIF. Currently, 50% of the value of the LIRA can be unlocked and changed back to RSP at the time of converting to a LIF. There are many other options that should be considered, which may or may not be available depending on your province of residence.

RIF – Retirement Income Fund

This is where an RRSP grows up to become an income. All RSP have to be converted to RIF by the end of the year the holder turns 71. These accounts have minimum amounts that must be withdrawn each year, but no maximum. They can be created from an RSP at any time but incomes, once started, cannot be stopped after age 71.

OPEN / Non-Registered

Type of investment vehicle that is OPEN, available or accessible at anytime. Not registered as an RRSP, TFSA, LIRA, LIF, etc. The account that is everything else. The catch-all investment type. It is important to understand that, unlike other types of registered investments, the taxable nature of what you hold inside these accounts determines the tax payable.

Different investments create different types of taxable income.

TFSA – Tax Free Savings Account

The worst named but best invention by the Canadian Government in years. Should have been called the TFIA. 'I' being for Investment, instead of 'S' being for Savings. But the 'T' and 'F' are 100% true! A great, very necessary addition to everyone's financial plan. But just like the door crashers on Black Friday, get one before they are gone. Never know how long something like this will be around.

AA – Accumulation Annuity

The insurance companies' version of the GIC. The basis of the AA estate plan and probably the best kept secret in the arena of guaranteed investment financial planning.

GIC – Guaranteed Interest Certificate

The guaranteed investment option that falls under The Bank Act. Can be properly used in OPEN accounts by those who hold them jointly, with rights of survivorship or registered money with those who have a spouse that haven't rolled over too.

POA - Power of Attorney

A document that gives someone else the ability to effectively clone you. Okay, maybe not clone, but almost. Legal documents that come in two distinct versions: Health and Stuff.

These documents give someone the ability to act as you when dealing with your **Stuff** or speak for you when you cannot when it comes to your **Health.** Proper names are the Power of Attorney for Property and Power of Attorney for Personal Care. Some provinces differ in how they refer to this type of document. For example, British Columbia calls it a Representative Agreement.

Executor

The person who executes the instructions set out in your will. This person should not be chosen the same way you choose a Best Man or Maid of Honour. A very important job that comes with much responsibility and liability.

Trustee

The person who administers the assets left in trust for beneficiaries either during your life (*inter vivos* trust) or after your death (testamentary trust). Also used to refer to an executor in some cases.

Beneficiary

The person or persons who will receive the value of a trust, life insurance, estate or certain investments.

Probate Tax

A levy (tax) on the value of your estate. With proper planning, this can be reduced and in some cases removed completely, so it never needs to be paid.

Life Changing Event

Common events that should trigger you to revisit your financial plan. They include, but are not limited to, weddings, birth of a child, family death, home purchase, job change, divorce and any substantial changes to a business you own.

Financial Plan

A living, breathing document that outlines your life path and how it integrates with your finances. To be started as young as possible, reviewed regularly and updated at each life changing event.

ABOUT THE AUTHOR

Bill McBay has enjoyed a successful career as a financial advisor since 1997. From that time till today, his favourite part of his role is getting to know clients on a personal level and providing them with the knowledge to help them achieve their financial goals and dreams.

His firm's name, T.E.A.M. Financial Solutions, an acronym for ***To Educate and Mentor,*** reflects this philosophy. He believes people make the best decisions when they fully understand all their options and can make an educated choice.

Bill has created various tools to help clients manage their financial lives. As well as this book, he has created a five-week retirement planning course, which turns common retirement planning exercises into a mock game show that gets everyone involved. Estate planning is Bill's passion, and he focuses on making the process enjoyable and easily understood so that clients can be confident in the decisions they make about their financial future.

Bill also delivers educational seminars to clients, employees and fellow advisors. He is often asked to speak to groups of his peers to help better the industry by educating advisors in how to operate a successful and compliant financial planning practice.

When not in his office, he enjoys giving back to his community. In 2010 he chartered the Kin Club of Woolwich, which raises money for the community's greatest need. Bill enjoys everything outdoors and finds cooking over an open fire very relaxing and a great way to have lots of friends around for some reason. 😆

Talk to Bill today about how he can provide you with the knowledge and power to help you achieve lifetime financial security. Together, you will create a personalized financial strategy to help you build your savings, protect yourself from the unexpected and retire *your* way with confidence. His long- standing relationships with clients are built on the highest level of service and his track record of helping people achieve their goals.

You can reach Bill McBay through his website at www.Bill-McBay.com